Growing God's Way

to see and share

V. GILBERT BEERS
RONALD A. BEERS

VICTOR BOOKS®
A DIVISION OF SCRIPTURE PRESS PUBLICATIONS INC.
USA CANADA ENGLAND

ARTISTS
    Ann Iosa
    Robert Korta
    Luciana Peters
    Blanche Sims
    Suzanne Snider

Copyright © 1987 by V. Gilbert Beers and Ronald A. Beers

Illustrations, copyright © by Scripture Press Publications, Inc. 1984

All rights in this book are reserved by the publishers, and no part may be reproduced without written permission, except for brief quotations in reviews.

Library of Congress Catalog Card Number: 87-81011
ISBN: 89693-801-8

Manufactured in the United States of America

To Parents and Teachers

Today your child will grow one day older. No matter what you do or don't do, time will not wait, and tomorrow your child will be physically one step closer toward adult maturity.

There is little you can do as parents or teachers to slow down or speed up the physical growth process. Assuming proper diet, exercise, rest, and health habits, physical growth is a steady day-by-day progress.

But what about the rest of your child's growth—mental, social, moral, and spiritual? These don't "just happen." It is your responsibility to see that these keep pace with physical growth in your child's life. Each day, each week, each month, and each year you want your child to grow God's way. You can't go back to "make up" for lost growth.

Growing God's way is what this book is all about. We could *tell you how* to help your child grow God's way. There are good books that do this, and we hope you read them and follow helpful advice. But this is not a how-to book.

GROWING GOD'S WAY is a book of delightful times with family and friends which will help your child grow the way God wants. You will want to do some of these things with your child, as well as read about them and talk about them. This book encourages your child to stop often and thank God for each special experience that helps him or her grow God's way.

These fun-filled experiences are so simple that we often pass them by in our hurried lives. But they are the building blocks of life for a growing child. They are also rich in imagination, with sights and sounds and smells everywhere.

Start now and watch your child grow God's way.

Growing God's Way to see and share

Contents

AFRAID: When you are afraid, remember that God is with you **81, 155**

AFRAID: God wants us to learn to be brave, but there are times when we should be afraid **109, 128**

ANIMALS: God made many animals for us to enjoy **103**

AUTUMN: God gives us four seasons each year, and autumn is one of those special times **135**

BAD DAYS: God helps us learn to do good things on rainy days **19**

BED: God gave us nice warm beds **167**

BIBLE: God has special ways to talk to us **71**

BIBLE: God gave us a special Book to help us grow His way **110, 111**

BIBLE-TIME: Growing up time is also Bible-time and prayertime **48**

BIRDS: God gives us birds to enjoy **98, 165**

BIRTH: God planned for some babies to come from eggs, and some to be born **34, 120**

BIRTHDAY: Each birthday reminds us that God made us and takes care of us **38**

BRAVE: God wants us to learn to be brave, but there are times when we should be afraid **81, 109, 128**

BROTHERS, SISTERS: God gives us brothers and sisters to grow up with us **43, 123**

CHRISTMAS: Christmas is a most wonderful time of the year **177**

CHURCH: We grow to love God at His house **61**

CHURCH: *We like to go to God's house as a family* **62**

CLEAN: *God wants us to be neat and clean* **107**

CLOTHING: *God gives us clothes* **39, 85, 94, 174**

COLD: *We should be thankful for cold and hot* **92**

COLORS: *God helps us see many beautiful colors* **75, 119**

CREATION: *God made many wonderful things and many wonderful places for us to enjoy* **89, 98, 99, 124, 158, 163**

CREATIVITY: *It's fun to make something special* **105**

DAUGHTER, MOTHER: *God is pleased when mothers and daughters make things together* **171**

DIFFERENT: *God made different kinds of animals and people* **116**

DRINK: *God gives us good things to drink* **84**

EGGS: *Some animal babies come from eggs* **34**

EYES: *We should look at things that help us grow God's way* **36**

EYES: *God gives us many beautiful things to see* **70, 75, 78**

FACE: *Our faces often tell people that we are growing God's way* **104**

FAMILIES: *God wants families to grow God's way by having good times together* **35, 57, 112, 117, 140, 168, 181**

FAMILY: *Be sure to tell family members you love them* **132**

FATHER, MOTHER: *God helps us grow up like Father or Mother* **12, 47**

FATHER, MOTHER: *It's fun to grow up with a father and mother who love each other* **59**

FATHER, MOTHER: *God gives us fathers and mothers to help us grow His way* **64, 91**

FATHER, MOTHER: *We are glad when Mother or Father is with us* **97**

FINGERS: *God gives us 10 fingers to help us grow His way* **40**

FOLLOW: *God wants us to learn to follow Him* **88**

FOOD: *God gives us good food to help us grow* **15, 24, 66, 73, 100, 138, 139**

FOOD: *God gives us special food for special times or places* **49, 50, 69, 79, 131, 143, 170**

FOOD: *Our bodies need food each day, and God helps us get it* **56, 134**

FOOD: *God gives each of His creatures a special kind of food* **86**

FOOD: *It is fun to eat with friends* **125**

FRIENDS: *Good friends will help us grow God's way* **53**

FRIENDS: *God wants us to have fun with our friends* **180**

GARDEN: *God helps our garden grow, and that*

helps us grow too **25**
GIFTS: *God gives us many special gifts* **82**
GIFTS: *God wants us to give good gifts to each other* **169, 172, 178**
GIVING: *God has given much to us, so we should give our best to Him* **133**
GOD: *God is with us each day as we grow* **26**
GOD'S HOUSE: *We grow to love God at His house* **61**
GOD'S HOUSE: *We like to go to God's house as a family* **62**
GRANDPARENTS: *God gives us grandparents to help us grow His way* **27, 63, 118, 153, 166**
GRASS: *God gives us grass to enjoy* **99**
GROWING: *New shoes and new clothing remind us how much we are growing* **150**
HANDS: *God wants us to use our hands to do good things for Him* **182**
HEALING: *We are glad that God helps us get well when we get hurt* **67**
HEARING: *We hear many wonderful sounds that help us grow God's way* **126, 175**
HELPING: *Growing God's way is learning to help others* **31, 68, 156**
HOMES: *God gives us good homes where we can grow* **28**
HOT: *We should be thankful for hot and cold* **92**

HURT: *God takes care of His people when others want to hurt them* **51**
HURT: *God helps us get well when we get hurt* **67**
JESUS: *Jesus helps us know God* **146**
JESUS: *Jesus knows what is best for us so we should obey Him* **151**
JESUS: *We grow God's way when we know that Jesus is alive and helping us* **33**
JESUS: *Jesus is with me wherever I go* **161**
KIND: *God wants us to be kind to each other* **145, 148**
LEARNING: *God teaches us special things* **77**
LOVE: *Growing God's way is knowing that someone special loves us* **29**
LOVE: *Growing God's way is loving special people and special things* **9, 130**
LOVE: *Special letters remind us that someone loves us* **46**
LOVE: *Be sure to tell family members that you love them* **132, 144**
MOON: *God made a beautiful moon to give us light at night* **72**
MORNING: *God wants us to be thankful for each new day* **90**
MOTHER, DAUGHTER: *God is pleased when mothers and daughters make things together* **171**
MOTHER, FATHER: *God helps us grow up like*

Mother or Father **12, 47**

MOTHER, FATHER: *It's fun to grow up with a mother and father who love each other* **59**

MOTHER, FATHER: *God gives us fathers and mothers to help us grow His way* **64, 91, 157, 164**

MOTHER, FATHER: *We grow best when mothers and fathers show us how to do things* **93, 154**

MOTHER, FATHER: *We are glad when Mother or Father is with us and helps us* **97, 147**

MOTHER, FATHER: *We learn from Mother and Father how to make special things* **154**

MUSIC: *God made music so we can praise Him with it* **42, 114, 176**

NOSE: *God gave us noses to help us smell good things* **52, 106**

OBEY: *Learning to obey is part of growing God's way* **14, 23, 76**

OTHERS: *We grow God's way as we learn to do things with others* **159**

OTHERS: *We grow God's way as we learn to help others* **160**

PARENTS: *(See also Mother and Father, or Father and Mother.) God has planned for us to do good things with our parents* **136, 149**

PLAY: *God gives us playtime to help us grow* **87, 113**

PLAY: *God gives us someone to play with us* **108**

PLAY: *God gives us fresh air outdoors, where we can play* **179**

PLEASING GOD: *Growing God's way is going where God wants and doing what God wants* **173**

PRAYERTIME: *Growing-up time is also Bible-time and prayertime* **48**

PRAYING: *We grow God's way when we talk often with Jesus* **21, 127**

PROTECT: *God sends special people to protect us* **122**

RAIN: *God sends rain to help things grow* **11**

RAINY DAY: *God helps us do good things indoors on a rainy day* **32**

SAFE: *God helps us keep safe* **83**

SEASONS: *God gives us four seasons each year* **135, 137, 141**

SEEDS: *God helps seeds grow into plants that give us good things* **17, 121**

SEEING: *God gives us many beautiful things to see* **70, 75, 78**

SHAPES: *God makes many special shapes* **119**

SHARING: *Growing God's way is learning to share* **30**

SISTERS, BROTHERS: *God gives us sisters and brothers to grow up with us* **43, 123**

SLEEP: *God gave us a special time to sleep and a special time to get up* **44**

SLEEP: *God gives us sleep, which helps us grow strong* **54**

SMELL: *God gives us noses to help us smell good things* **52, 106, 129**

SPRING: *God helps special things grow in the springtime* **13**

STARS: *God put beautiful stars in the sky for us to enjoy* **58**

STORES: *We should be glad for stores where we can buy things to help us grow* **60**

TAKE CARE OF: *God has special ways to take care of us while we grow up* **45, 95**

TAKE CARE OF: *Father or Mother will not let us fall, and neither will God* **80**

TASTE: *God helps us taste good things* **55, 74, 129**

TEETH: *God gives us good teeth to help us grow His way* **41**

THANKFUL: *We learn to be thankful when we see special things God has done for us* **96**

TIME: *God wants us to learn to tell time so that we can use the time He gives us wisely* **162**

TIME: *We learn God plans for seasons* **18**

TOGETHER: *We are glad when we can be together with those we love* **152**

TOYS: *We should thank God for bedtime friends who help us sleep well* **37**

WATER: *God gives us water to help us grow* **20, 102**

WILDFLOWERS: *Wildflowers remind us that God takes care of us while we grow* **22**

WIND: *We should be thankful for growing-up times on a windy day* **10, 16**

WORK: *God planned for each of us to find a special way to earn a living* **115**

WORK: *God wants us to have fun together as we work* **142**

WORLD: *God wants us to love other people around the world* **65**

Writing to Someone You Love

***Growing God's Way:** God gives us a family to love us. We should remember to talk with them or write to them.*

What do you think this girl and boy are doing? Are they sending Christmas cards? Is it Easter time? Why not? What do you see that tells you it is some other special time of the year? The boy is writing a note on his valentine. He is telling Grandmother and Grandfather that he loves them. Do you think they will be glad to read that? God tells us in the Bible that He loves us. Aren't you glad to know that He loves you?

A TIME TO SHARE

1. *What are the boy and girl doing?*
2. *Whose picture do you see?*
3. *How will they know the boy loves them?*
4. *Would you like to thank God now for family members who love you?*

WHAT DO YOU SEE?

How many pencils does this boy have? Can you find them? What month is this? Point to something that tells you. Find four people that this boy loves very much.

Who Sends the Wind?

Growing God's Way: We learn to thank God for the wind that He made.

Can you feel the wind blowing? How does it feel when it blows on your face? The wind brings the clouds that give you rain. Wind sighs in the trees and tugs at your kite to make it go up in the sky. Aren't you glad that you can fly your kite with Father? Aren't you glad that God sends the wind?

WHAT DO YOU SEE?
Point to some things that blow in the wind. What keeps the kite from blowing away? How many kites can you find?

A TIME TO SHARE
1. How do you know the wind is blowing?
2. Who sends the wind?
3. Would you like to thank God now for the wind that blows your kite and brings the clouds with rain?

Raindrops and Puddles

Growing God's Way: ***We thank God for rain that helps things grow.***

You can see that the rain is over. Now it is time to splash in this puddle. God sends the rain to make things grow. If He did not give us rain, we would have no green grass or trees or flowers. If God did not give us rain, food would not grow. What would we eat then? The girl and the boys are glad God sends the rain to make things grow. They're glad they can splash in puddles too!

A TIME TO SHARE
1. *What made these puddles?*
2. *What does the rain do for us?*
3. *How does the rain tell you that God loves you?*
4. *How would you like to thank God now for rain that makes food grow?*

WHAT DO YOU SEE?
How do you know that it has just rained? Point to some things that you see on a rainy day.

God Planned for Me to Grow

Growing God's Way: God planned for baby chicks to grow and for children too.

Have you ever held a baby chick? This girl thinks the chick is soft and fluffy. But do you see the mother hen? She is not soft and fluffy, is she? She is not tiny like the baby chick. One day the baby chick will grow up and become a mother hen or a rooster. It will not be soft and fluffy then. The little girl will also grow up and be like her mother. That's the way God planned it. He planned for baby chicks to grow up. And He planned for boys and girls to grow up too. Aren't you glad God planned for you to grow?

WHAT DO YOU SEE?
Point to some things that tell you this is a farm. Can you count the chicks? How many are there?

A TIME TO SHARE
1. Why is the hen bigger than the chicks?
2. Why is mother bigger than the girl?
3. How will the chicks grow? How will the girl grow? Who planned it this way?

WHAT DO YOU SEE?
How many daffodils do you see? What color are they? What else do you see that you did not see last winter?

God Gives Us Daffodils

Growing God's Way: We are thankful for the daffodils that God sends in the spring.

Now here is something you didn't see last winter! You know it's spring when daffodils bloom in your backyard and robins come back. Mother smiles because she remembers planting strange brown bulbs last fall. They didn't look like yellow daffodils then. But God sent the warm sun and rain. Now look what came from those brown bulbs. God gives us many things in the spring. God has promised to send spring and fall, summer and winter. He does this every year. He will do it next year too. He will never forget, will He?

A TIME TO SHARE
1. *What did Mother plant last fall?*
2. *What came from those strange brown bulbs?*
3. *What will God do for us each spring?*
4. *Will He ever forget to do this?*

Why Should I Obey?

Growing God's Way: We want to obey God as Noah did.

Look at that big boat. God told Noah to make it. The boat will keep Noah and his family safe from a big flood. Noah could have said no. He did not have to obey God. But he did. Now he and his family are safe. They are thanking God for keeping them safe from the big flood. Don't you think Noah and his family are glad they obeyed God?

A TIME TO SHARE
1. *Why did Noah make the big boat?*
2. *What could have happened if he had not obeyed God?*
3. *Why should you obey God? Why should you obey parents?*

WHAT DO YOU SEE?
How many people do you see here? Which do you think is Noah? Point to the altar. People burned a sacrifice on an altar at that time. It was one way of saying thank you to God. What kept Noah and his family safe from the flood? Point to it.

Growing with God's Good Food

Growing God's Way: We grow strong by eating the good food God gives us.

Do you see what the boy is holding in his hand? It is an apple, isn't it? God made apples for us to eat, didn't He? He made other good food too. God's good food helps us grow strong and keeps us healthy. Are you glad God made good food for you to eat? Do you thank Him before you eat the good food He gives you?

A TIME TO SHARE
1. *How many boys and girls do you see?*
2. *What are they doing?*
3. *Could they eat lunch if God did not give them good food?*
4. *What should they do before they eat?*

WHAT DO YOU SEE?
What time of day is this? How do you know? How do you know these boys and girls are at school? How do you know this is not breakfast?

Do You Hear God's Wind?

Growing God's Way: We grow to love God with a fun day in the wind.

This looks like a fun day to be outside! You can see that it is a windy day. But how could the boy fly his kite if it were not windy? How could the girls watch the leaves blow? The wind sighing in the leaves sounds like the trees are whispering. Do you like to play outside on a windy day? What fun things can you do on a windy day?

WHAT DO YOU SEE?
Point to six things blowing in the wind. How would each of these look if the wind were not blowing?

A TIME TO SHARE
1. *Who sends the wind?*
2. *Why does God send the wind?*
3. *Why are you thankful for the wind?*

How Does Your Garden Grow?

Growing God's Way: When seeds grow, you know that God is helping them as He helps us.

Spring is here. You wouldn't see this family planting seeds in the winter, would you? You wouldn't see them planting in the fall either. Spring is the right time to plant a garden. Look at Father. What is he doing? Do you like to dig up the dirt in your garden? Father does. Mother makes a place for the seeds. Then the boy and girl will plant them. Before long you will see plants growing. God will give this family good food from these plants.

WHAT DO YOU SEE?
Is this summer, spring, or winter? How do you know? Point to some seeds. What will grow from them? Good food will help the boy and girl to grow stronger, like Mother and Father.

A TIME TO SHARE
1. *What are these people planting?*
2. *Who makes the seeds grow?*
3. *What will God give from these seeds?*
4. *Do you thank God for good food?*

God Sends Robins in the Spring

Growing God's Way: We learn God plans for spring, summer, autumn, and winter.

Look! Do you see the robin sitting outside the window? This family sees it. They are glad. This bird comes back only when winter is gone. That's when God wants it to do this. When a robin hops on your lawn, you know that spring has come. God sends robins in the spring. This is part of God's plan for the seasons.

WHAT DO YOU SEE?
What do you see that says spring? Who is inside the house?

A TIME TO SHARE
1. *What do you see here that tells you it is spring?*
2. *Who gives us the different seasons?*
3. *Can you name the four seasons? How much older are you when all four seasons have come?*

I'm Glad for a Rainy Day

Growing God's Way: Learning to do good things when the day is not so good.

Do you like a rainy day? This girl does. She and her mother are going downtown. They like to walk in the rain. But what keeps them from getting wet? Mother has brought her umbrella. Now she and the girl can walk and not get wet. Do you like to do good things on rainy days like this?

A TIME TO SHARE
1. *Why does God send rain?*
2. *Do you ever grumble when God sends a rainy day?*
3. *What good things can you do on a rainy day like this?*

WHAT DO YOU SEE?
How do you know that it is raining? Point to something that would stop growing if it did not rain.

What Do You Get from a Well?

***Growing God's Way:** God gives us water to help us grow.*

Isaac did not have electric pumps. He did not have faucets and sinks and bathtubs. Isaac and his friends had to dig wells to get water. They have just finished digging this one. Now they are putting stones around the top. The place where Isaac lived did not have much water. Wells were very important. How can you live without water?

A TIME TO SHARE
1. *What are these men doing?*
2. *What will they get from this well?*
3. *Why were wells so important then?*
4. *Why does God give us water each day?*

WHAT DO YOU SEE?
How many men are working on this well? Point to things that will die without water. God gives us water to keep us alive. Would you like to thank Him?

A Time to Talk with Jesus

Growing God's Way: We grow God's way when we talk with Jesus.

How would you feel if you could never talk with Mother or Father? How would you feel if you could never talk with Jesus? Prayertime is a special time, isn't it? This girl is glad that she can talk with Jesus. She is glad that she has this special time just before bedtime. Do you like to talk with Jesus just before bedtime?

A TIME TO SHARE
1. *What is this girl doing?*
2. *Father is standing, Mother is sitting, and the girl is kneeling. Are they all praying? Can you pray in any of these ways?*

WHAT DO YOU SEE?
What room is this? How do you know? Who is standing? Who is sitting? Who is kneeling?

Something You Don't Have to Plant

Growing God's Way: God helps the wildflowers grow, and He helps you grow too.

Do you see what the girl is giving to Father? Those are called wildflowers. She did not plant them. Father did not plant them. No one else planted them. God put them there in the woods. God causes many flowers and bushes and trees to grow. He lets us see them. He lets us touch them. He lets us smell them. But we did not have to plant them. Do you thank God for wildflowers and plants and trees?

A TIME TO SHARE
1. *What is the girl giving to Father?*
2. *Who planted the wildflowers?*
3. *How does God help the wildflowers grow? How does He help you grow?*

WHAT DO YOU SEE?
Do you think this is in the city? Why not? Where do you think Father and the girl are today? How do you know the girl is happy to be there?

Learning to Obey

Growing God's Way: We grow to please God when we learn to obey God and parents.

Look who is driving the car. Do you think Father can do anything he wants when he is driving? Father will tell you that there are many laws. He must obey them. If he doesn't, a policeman will stop him. He will tell Father to obey the laws. Even fathers must learn to obey. Don't you think you need to obey too?

A TIME TO SHARE
1. *Can Father do anything he wants?*
2. *Must fathers learn to obey too?*
3. *Why must you learn to obey? Who should you obey?*

WHAT DO YOU SEE?
How fast is Father going? Why do you think this is not faster than the speed limit? What else is Father doing to obey the law?

Who Gives You Food to Eat?
Growing God's Way: God gives us good food to help us grow.

What are these boys and this girl eating? Do you like to eat peanut butter? Do you like jam too? Ummm. You can taste it now, can't you? But who gives you good food to eat? What would happen if Mother or Father did not buy food for you? Where would you get it? What would happen if God did not make the food grow? Where would Mother or Father get food?

A TIME TO SHARE
1. *What are your favorite foods?*
2. *What plants or animals give you these foods?*
3. *Would the plants or animals grow without sunshine or rain?*
4. *Who sends the sunshine and rain?*

WHAT DO YOU SEE?
Name each food you see. You should find four. Point to each one. How many knives do you see? How many spoons?

A Friend Who Helps Your Garden Grow

Growing God's Way: God helps our garden grow, and that helps us grow too.

Here is a friend who won't argue with you! But he can't play with you either. This friend has a special job to do. Do you know what it is? He won't hoe the garden. He won't plant the seeds. He won't bring the vegetables into the house for you. But he will help your garden grow. When you eat peas or corn or tomatoes from your garden, remember your scarecrow friend. It's nice to have scarecrow friends, but let's remember that God makes the garden grow.

A TIME TO SHARE
1. *What work does the scarecrow do?*
2. *Does this help you have good food?*
3. *Who makes the garden grow?*

WHAT DO YOU SEE?
What is growing in this garden? Point to each kind of seed that is planted. How many girls do you see? How many boys?

Is God with You?

Growing God's Way: God is with us each day as we grow.

Have you ever seen angels walking on a stairway like this? Jacob had never seen anything like that before either. God gave Jacob a dream about angels walking on these long steps. They are going up and down between Jacob and heaven. What would you think if you dreamed of angels? In his dream, God told Jacob that He was there with him. God does not need to send a dream like this to you. He tells you in the Bible that He is with you. The Bible is His special letter to you.

WHAT DO YOU SEE?
What is this man doing? How many angels do you see? How many are coming down the stairway? How many are going up?

A TIME TO SHARE
1. Who is sleeping here?
2. Who is on the stairway?
3. Is God here with Jacob? Is He with you? How do you know?

Whose Attic Is This?

Growing God's Way: God gives us grandmas and grandpas to help us grow.

Look! Who do you think wore that hat before it was put into the attic? Do you think the girl wore it? Do you think the boy wore it? Grandma's attic is a special place, isn't it? But that's because Grandma is a special person. Do you have a special grandma or grandpa? God gave us grandmas and grandpas as part of His plan. Have you ever thanked Him for your grandma or grandpa?

WHAT DO YOU SEE?
Point to some of the things in Grandma's attic. What did Grandma do with each one? How do you know this is an attic and not a basement?

A TIME TO SHARE
1. *Whose attic is this?*
2. *Why do you think it is Grandma's?*
3. *Why do you think Grandma loves the boy and girl? Why do you think God loves the boy and girl?*

Something Outside My Window

Growing God's Way: God gives good homes to birds and to us.

What is that bird doing outside the window? Do you see the home it has made in the tree? It is called a nest. There is something special in the nest. Do you know what it is? Do you know what the mother bird is giving to her baby? But how does the mother bird know what to do? Who tells her how to make a nest home and feed the babies?

A TIME TO SHARE
1. What kind of home does the bird have?
2. Why would that not be a good home for you? Why would your home not be a good home for the bird?

WHAT DO YOU SEE?
Which room of the house is this? How do you know? Is the bird's nest inside the boy's house or outside? How do you know?

Someone Who Makes Me Happy

Growing God's Way: We are happy when we know someone special loves us.

Why does Kitty look so happy? Kitty knows the girl loves her. You can see that too, can't you? Do you suppose the girl is happy because she knows Father loves her? Someone else loves this girl. Do you know who He is?

A TIME TO SHARE
1. Why do you think Kitty is happy?
2. Why do you think the girl is happy?
3. How do you know that Father loves her?
4. How do you know that Jesus loves her?

WHAT DO YOU SEE?
How many frowns do you see? How many happy faces do you see?

Sharing Something Special

Growing God's Way: God wants us to share special things with others.

This boy has found something special. Do you see what it is? The boy has never seen such a beautiful moth before. He wants to share it with Mother and Father. "Come and see what I found," he tells them. When you find something special, do you like to share it with someone you love? Is that why you like to tell others about Jesus?

A TIME TO SHARE
1. *What has the boy found?*
2. *Why is he calling Mother and Father?*
3. *Why should we share special things?*
4. *Why should we tell others about Jesus?*

WHAT DO YOU SEE?
Where is this family? Are they on a city street? Point to some things that tell you where they are. Is this a spring day or a winter day? Point to some things that tell you which kind of day it is.

Helping Those We Love

Growing God's Way: *God wants us to help those we love.*

Have you ever seen your mother do this? This boy's mother is sewing a button on his shirt. But why doesn't she tell the boy to sew his own button? Do you suppose Mother wants to do this for her boy? Do you suppose she helps him because she loves him? Aren't you glad for all the special things Mother does for you?

A TIME TO SHARE
1. *What is Mother doing?*
2. *Name five special things Mother does for you.*
3. *Why does she do these things for you?*
4. *Would you like to thank her now?*

WHAT DO YOU SEE?
Name each thing Mother uses when she sews the button on the boy's shirt. What does she do with each?

A Rainy Day Is Fun Too

Growing God's Way: God helps us do good things indoors on a rainy day.

Do you like to watch the raindrops come down? It's fun if you are inside, looking out. But it's not so much fun for that man outside. The wind is blowing and the rain is pouring down. He's hurrying to get home. He wants to get out of the rain. But look at the boy by the window. He is not hurrying to get outside, is he? He will find some good things to do inside on a rainy day. Do you like to do that?

WHAT DO YOU SEE?
How do you know it is raining? What would the boy have to put on if he went outside now?

A TIME TO SHARE
1. *Who sends the rain?*
2. *What do you like to do on a rainy day?*
3. *Do you thank God for a warm, dry house where you can play on a rainy day?*

The Tomb Is Empty

Growing God's Way: *We are glad that Jesus is alive and wants to be our Friend.*

That big stone is taller than you. Someone worked hard to make it round. That's so people could roll it in front of the cave. Jesus was buried in that cave. But He is not there now! He came back to life and came out of the cave. Jesus went back to heaven. You can talk to Him now. He is alive. Aren't you glad Jesus is alive?

WHAT DO YOU SEE?
Point to the cave where Jesus was buried. Point to the stone that covered the cave.

A TIME TO SHARE
1. *Who was in that cave?*
2. *Why is He not there now?*
3. *Where is He today?*
4. *Why are you glad Jesus is alive?*

Some Babies Come from Eggs

Growing God's Way: God planned for some babies to come from eggs.

Do you like to color eggs? When do you do this? Is it Christmas? Is it Thanksgiving? Is it Easter? It's fun to color eggs. It's fun to eat them too. Sometimes mother chickens sit on eggs for a long time. Then the shell breaks open. A new baby chick comes out. God planned for some babies to come from eggs.

WHAT DO YOU SEE?
How many eggs can you count? What colors do you see? Do you see something else that lays eggs? Point to them. Kitty sees them!

A TIME TO SHARE
1. *Why do people color eggs at Easter?*
2. *What else do you do with eggs?*
3. *What kind of babies come from eggs like these?*

Doing Things Together

Growing God's Way: God wants families to have good times together.

This family is ready to do something special. They will do it together. The picnic basket is almost ready. Father and the boy are checking the map. They want to be sure they know which way to go. Do you think they will have fun on their trip? Do you think Someone else will be with them? Who is always with them?

A TIME TO SHARE
1. What is this family going to do?
2. Which of them will go on the trip?
3. Who will be with them?

WHAT DO YOU SEE?
Where is the map? Point to it. What does the map tell Father and the boy? God tells us many things in the Bible. How is the Bible like a map?

Thank You for My Eyes

***Growing God's Way:** We should thank God for eyes to see good things.*

I have two eyes. How many do you have? Puppy has two eyes too! But Father teases me. He says he has four eyes. Do you know what he means? You can see Father sitting there in his chair. He is reading his newspaper. But he cannot read it well with only his two eyes. Some friends at school have glasses too. They are glad for glasses to help them read. They are glad for their eyes too. Are you? If you are glad, remember who gave them to you.

WHAT DO YOU SEE?
How many eyes do you see in this picture? Point to each one.

A TIME TO SHARE
1. *What are five things you see now?*
2. *Why do you think God gave you eyes? Are you glad that He did?*
3. *Would you like to thank God now for your eyes?*

Bedtime Friends

***Growing God's Way:** We should thank God for bedtime friends who help us sleep well.*

This girl has lots of bedtime friends. Can you count them? Don't forget Mother. She is a good bedtime friend. Mother tells the girl a story about God at bedtime. She prays with the girl too. The girl has one bedtime friend you cannot see. Do you know who He is?

A TIME TO SHARE
1. *Who is the bedtime Friend you can't see?*
2. *How do you know God is with you?*
3. *Do you like to talk with God at bedtime? What do you like to say to Him?*

WHAT DO YOU SEE?
Point to each stuffed animal and tell what it is. Point to the one you think is her favorite.

Birthday Party

Growing God's Way: Each birthday reminds us that God made us and takes care of us.

Would you like to come to this boy's birthday party? He's a year older today. You can see how old he is by counting the candles. How many did you find? Each year God helps us grow the way we should at that age. Aren't you glad God has a special plan for us each year? This boy will thank God tonight for his birthday. Would you like to thank God tonight for His special plan for you this year?

WHAT DO YOU SEE?
Point to each thing that tells you this is a birthday party and not a Christmas party. Can you name each one?

A TIME TO SHARE
1. *How old is this boy? Should he act and talk like a two-year-old? Why not?*
2. *Who gives us a special plan for each year of our lives? Have you thanked Him?*

A Beautiful Coat

Growing God's Way: God gives us clothes to wear.

This young man is glad for his beautiful coat. You can see that, can't you? But you wouldn't be glad for Joseph's coat, would you? You and your friends do not dress like that. In Bible days, Joseph and his friends dressed this way. Anyone was glad for a beautiful new coat. But not many young men got a coat as nice as this. It was better than others. That's because Joseph's father wanted to tell Joseph how much he loved him. He wanted to tell others that he loved Joseph more than any other son.

WHAT DO YOU SEE?
How is Joseph's clothing different from yours? How is Joseph's home different from yours? Are you as thankful as Joseph for home and clothes?

A TIME TO SHARE
1. What special gift does Joseph have?
2. Who did he thank for it?
3. *Do you thank your parents for clothes?*
4. *Do you thank God for clothes?*

Thank You, God, for Fingers

Growing God's Way: God gives us 10 fingers to help us grow.

Do you see this busy family? There is Father, writing something at his desk. Mother is sewing. But what are the girl and the boy doing? Are these people using their toes or their fingers? Could Puppy play the piano or sew? Could he write a letter? Why not? Tonight each of these people will say "thank You, God, for fingers." Do you know why?

WHAT DO YOU SEE?
How many fingers do all of these people have? How many fingers does Puppy have? How does he pick up his bone?

A TIME TO SHARE
1. *Think of five things you do with your fingers. Could you do them without fingers? Why not?*
2. *What can you do that Puppy can't do?*
3. *Will you thank God for your fingers?*

Do You Brush Your Teeth?

Growing God's Way: God gives you good teeth to help you eat your food.

Do you brush your teeth? Of course you do. This girl does each morning. She does again before she goes to bed at night. Sometimes she likes to brush her teeth after she eats. It feels good to get that furry stuff from your teeth, doesn't it? Toothpaste tastes good too. Do you like that minty taste? God gave you teeth to chew your food. Would you like to thank Him for good teeth? Why don't you do that each time you brush your teeth?

WHAT DO YOU SEE?
What room is this? Point to some things you have in your bathroom. How do you use each one?

A TIME TO SHARE
1. *What is this girl doing? Why?*
2. *Why doesn't Kitty need to do this?*
3. *Who gave you good teeth? Why should you keep them clean?*

Listen to My Music

Growing God's Way: God helps you make music for others to enjoy.

Do you think this girl is having fun? When she hits the right keys, the boy hears music. Do you think he likes the girl's music? The girl is playing the notes for "Jesus Loves Me, This I Know." When the boy hears these notes he thinks about the words. He and the girl may even sing those words. Would you like to hear them?

WHAT DO YOU SEE?
How many keys do you see on this xylophone? How does the girl make music on this instrument? Which musical instruments do you have in your house? Do you play one?

A TIME TO SHARE
1. *What instrument is the girl playing?*
2. *What song is she playing?*
3. *What special songs about Jesus do you like to sing?*

A Special Day

Growing God's Way: God gives us brothers and sisters to grow up with us.

Look at this happy family! The boy and girl have a new baby sister. This is the first time they have seen her. It is a special day, isn't it? Father is happy. You can see that, can't you? Mother is happy too. But you can't see her now. Do you know why? In a few days this family will take their new baby home. Then the boy and girl can hold their new baby sister. Do you think they will thank God for giving her to their family?

A TIME TO SHARE
1. *Why is this a special day?*
2. *Why is each person happy today?*
3. *Why should this family thank God for the new baby?*

WHAT DO YOU SEE?
Where is this family? Is it the grocery store? Why not? What kind of work do those two ladies do? Can you point to the place where the babies sleep?

Good Morning, Sunshine

Growing God's Way: There is a time to sleep and a time to get up.

"Good morning!" That's Mother peeking around the corner. It's time to get up. The sun is shining and Mother has breakfast ready. But this girl is a sleepyhead. She wants to stay in bed just a little longer. You know how she feels, don't you? Your bed is the warmest, coziest, snuggliest place of all. But this is a new day that God has given. There are many new things to do. The girl will have to get up if she wants to do them.

A TIME TO SHARE
1. Who sends each new day?
2. What are some good things you want to do today?
3. Can you do these if you stay in bed?

WHAT DO YOU SEE?
What time of day is it? How do you know? Which room is this? Point to some things that tell you that.

God Takes Care of Us

Growing God's Way: God has special ways to take care of us while we are growing up.

Look! Do you see that basket on the river? Baby Moses was in the basket. His mother put him there. She was hiding him from the wicked king. He wanted to kill all the Hebrew baby boys in Egypt. But look who found him. The princess is holding Baby Moses. She will not let the king hurt him. Now you know that God took care of Baby Moses. God takes care of you too.

A TIME TO SHARE
1. *Why did Baby Moses' mother hide him?*
2. *Why is he safe now?*
3. *How did God take care of Baby Moses?*
4. *How does God take care of you?*

WHAT DO YOU SEE?
What is in Baby Moses' basket now? Who was in it? Where is Baby Moses now? Do you think the princess is rich or poor? How do you know?

Something Says I Love You
Growing God's Way: Special letters remind us that someone loves us.

This girl is happy about something. Do you see what it is? Father has just come from the mailbox. The girl knows that she has just received a letter in the mail. It is from Grandfather and Grandmother. They will say something special to this girl. They will tell the girl how much they love her. The Bible is like this letter, isn't it? God tells us in the Bible how much He loves us. Aren't you glad that He does?

WHAT DO YOU SEE?
Can you find the mailbox where Father found the letter? Can you find the pictures of the people who sent it? How do you know the girl lives in the country?

A TIME TO SHARE
1. What is Father holding in his hand?
2. Who sent this special letter?
3. What did Grandmother and Grandfather say to the girl? How does God tell you that He loves you?

Growing Up to Be Like Mother

Growing God's Way: It is fun to think of growing up like Mother or Father.

Do you ever play dress-up? This girl does. You can see that she is wearing Mother's clothes. She is pretending that she is a mother. But she will have to grow up much more to be a mother, won't she? If she wants to be like Mother, she will read her Bible and pray every day. That's what Mother does. That's a good way to grow, isn't it?

WHAT DO YOU SEE?
Why do you think those are Mother's clothes on the girl? Why are they not the girl's clothes? Why are they not Father's clothes?

A TIME TO SHARE
1. *Whose clothes is the girl wearing?*
2. *Why does the girl want to be like Mother? What will she have to do to be like her?*

Special Times at Dinnertime

Growing God's Way: Growing up time is also Bible-time and prayertime.

This family has just finished dinner. But they are not ready to leave the table yet. Father has brought the Bible to the table. He will read something from the Bible. Then he and Mother and the boy will talk about it. After that, they will pray. They call this special time Bible-time. It is a special time at dinnertime. Do you think God is glad they are doing this?

WHAT DO YOU SEE?
What time is it? Why do you think this is evening and not morning? Why do you think dinner is over?

A TIME TO SHARE
1. *What is Father reading?*
2. *What else will this family do?*
3. *Why is Jesus pleased because the family has Bible-time?*

Time for Lunch

***Growing God's Way:** Be sure to thank God for special food, like lunch at school.*

Do you ever take your lunch to school? These boys and girls do. You can see they are eating food from their lunch boxes. But who put the lunches into their boxes? Do you think it was Mother or Father? Do you think these boys and girls are glad that Mother or Father gave them good food to eat? Do you think they are glad that God helped this good food grow?

A TIME TO SHARE
1. *What are these girls and boys eating?*
2. *Who gave them this good food? Who helped this good food to grow?*
3. *Do you remember to thank God for good food?*

WHAT DO YOU SEE?
What time does the clock show? Why is this not breakfast or dinnertime? Why do you think this is at school?

Do You Like Cherry Pie?

Growing God's Way: God gives wonderful fruits and berries for us to eat.

Now that dinner is over it's time for dessert. Tonight this boy is getting a favorite. You can see how happy he is to get it. Mother is happy to cut the hot cherry pie. Father is happy to put some vanilla ice cream on the pieces of pie. But this family would not have cherry pie unless God helped a cherry tree grow. They would not have ice cream unless God helped a cow give milk. Cherry pie with ice cream is really a cherry tree and a cow working together. God has some wonderful ways to give you food, doesn't He?

A TIME TO SHARE
1. *What is this family eating?*
2. *How did a cow and a cherry tree help the family have dessert?*
3. *How did God help them have dessert?*

WHAT DO YOU SEE?
Who is cutting the pie? Who is putting the ice cream on it? Who is going to eat it?

Who Wants to Hurt God's People?

Growing God's Way: *God takes care of His people when others want to hurt them.*

You wouldn't see this thing going down your street, would you? Your friends and neighbors drive cars or trucks or vans. But this man did not have any of those things. He was glad to have a chariot. Only rich men or important soldiers had chariots. This man knows there are enemy soldiers nearby. He is ready for them. He has an arrow to shoot. He knows God will keep him safe from the enemy.

A TIME TO SHARE
1. *What is this thing called?*
2. *What is the man doing with it?*
3. *What does this man know God will do for him?*

WHAT DO YOU SEE?
How many arrows can you find? You should find as many arrows as your fingers or toes.

Something Smells Good

Growing God's Way: *Aren't you glad God gave you a nose to smell good things?*

Have you ever seen your nose? You can't see all of it unless you look in a mirror. God made your nose in a special place on your face. It does not keep your eyes from seeing. God made your nose for something important. Could you smell Mother's perfume without your nose? Could you smell Thanksgiving dinner without it? Could you smell flowers or apples without it? Have you ever thanked God for your nose? Would you like to do that now?

A TIME TO SHARE
1. *How many things can you smell? Can you name five different things?*
2. *Which things do you not like to smell? Which do you like to smell best?*

WHAT DO YOU SEE?
Point to something the girl can smell now. Do you think Mother's perfume smells good?

Having Fun as We Grow Together

Growing God's Way: Good friends will help us grow God's way.

These three boys live near each other. You can see that they like to get together to play. But look at that one boy in the chair. Do you think he is having fun today? Perhaps he had a quarrel with his friends. Or he could be angry because he didn't win. The other two boys are having fun together, aren't they? Which is better, to have fun together or to quarrel with each other? Which pleases Jesus?

A TIME TO SHARE
1. *Who is having fun here?*
2. *Would you rather quarrel or have fun?*
3. *What would you like to say to the boy who is pouting in the chair?*

WHAT DO YOU SEE?
How many marbles do you see? You should find as many as the fingers on your right hand. What else can the boys play with? What can they do with each one?

God Gives Us Sleep

***Growing God's Way:** God gives us sleep to help us grow strong.*

How would you feel if you couldn't sleep at night? Would you feel tired and grumpy the next day? This girl looks happy, doesn't she? That's because she has slept well all night. Mother and Father are happy that she has slept well. They are happy because they slept well too. God gives us sleep. It's His way of helping us feel well and rested. Do you ever say "thank You, Lord, for sleep?"

WHAT DO YOU SEE?
How do you know this is morning and not noon? How do you know this is the girl's bedroom and not the kitchen?

A TIME TO SHARE
1. *Do you think this girl has slept well?*
2. *How would she feel if she had not slept well all night?*
3. *Who gives us sleep?*
4. *Would you like to thank Him now?*

Thank You, God, for Sweet Things

Growing God's Way: God helps us taste sweet things. Be sure to thank Him.

Look at all that wonderful candy! Can you find some peppermint sticks? Do you suppose there are chocolates and gumdrops too? Most boys and girls like to taste candy. It is sweet. Of course we need to be careful not to eat too much candy. That would not be good for us. God helps us taste different kinds of things. Some things are sweet. Other things are sour. Some are salty. Others are bitter. Aren't you glad God helps you taste different kinds of things?

A TIME TO SHARE
1. *Is candy sweet or sour? Is a pickle bitter or sour?*
2. *Can you name some things that are sour? Name some things that are sweet.*

WHAT DO YOU SEE?
How many kinds of candy do you see? Where will Mother find the money to buy something?

God Sends Food Each Day

Growing God's Way: Our bodies need food each day, and God gives us food.

Those white things are not snow. They are food called manna. The people of Israel were hungry. They did not have gardens. They did not have grocery stores. They were afraid they would die. But God sent the manna for them to eat. Every day He gave them manna. They never had to be hungry again. Does God give you food each day?

WHAT DO YOU SEE?
Point to the manna. How do you know it is good to eat? Where is the girl putting her manna? Where do you think she lives?

A TIME TO SHARE
1. Who sent this manna?
2. Why did God send it?
3. How often did God give His people food to eat?

Growing Together as a Family

Growing God's Way: God helps us grow up with others in a family. He knows that is a special way to grow up.

Would you like to grow up alone? That would not be fun, would it? This girl is happy that she has a mother and father. She is happy that her mother and father like to do things with her. Do you see what Mother is doing? Do you suppose she is reading this book to the girl? Do you think Mother is reading about Jesus to the girl?

WHAT DO YOU SEE?
How many smiles do you see? How many frowns do you see? Who is making someone happy? Find five things that you also have in your house.

A TIME TO SHARE
1. What is Mother doing?
2. Why do you think the girl is happy?
3. Do you like Mother or Father to read about Jesus? Why?

Will You Share My Stars?

Growing God's Way: God put beautiful stars in the sky for us to enjoy.

Look at all those beautiful stars! This girl wants to share them with Mother. That's the way it is when we find something wonderful, isn't it? We want to share it with someone we love. Do you think Mother shares good things with the girl? Do you think Jesus shares good things with Mother and the girl?

WHAT DO YOU SEE?
How do you know this is night? Is it late at night or early at night? Whose room is this? How can you tell?

A TIME TO SHARE
1. What does the girl see?
2. Why does she want to share them with Mother?
3. Why do you like to share good things?

58

A Ring on Your Finger

Growing God's Way: It's fun to grow up with a mother and father who love each other.

This girl is looking at something special. Do you see the ring? Father gave this ring to Mother when they were married. The ring reminds Mother and Father that they are married. It reminds them that they love each other. The girl is glad that Mother and Father love each other. She wants to grow up in a happy home. Don't you think she should be glad for that?

WHAT DO YOU SEE?
Is Mother smiling or frowning? Is the girl smiling or frowning? How do you know that Mother and the girl are happy?

A TIME TO SHARE
1. *What does the girl see?*
2. *Who gave the ring to Mother?*
3. *What does the ring help them remember?*
4. *Are you glad for a happy home?*

Stores That Sell Good Things

Growing God's Way: We should be glad for stores where we can buy things to help us grow.

Do you like to buy things at the store? Many people in the world do not have stores. Many do not have stores with food or candy or clothes. Mother buys your food at the grocery store. She buys your clothes at a clothing store. Can you think of other kinds of stores where you can buy things?

WHAT DO YOU SEE?
What kind of store is this? How do you know? Can you find peppermint sticks?

A TIME TO SHARE
1. Stores sell food and clothing. But all food and clothing comes from plants and animals. Who makes the plants and animals grow?
2. Do you thank God for things you buy?

God's House

Choosing God's Way: We grow to love God at His house.

Do you call your church God's house? Most people do. But look at this tent. Moses and his people called it God's house. God said they should. It was a special kind of tent. God told them how to make it. It was a wonderful place because it was so beautiful. But it was more wonderful because God was there. Is that why you love your church so much?

A TIME TO SHARE
1. *Why was this tent called God's house?*
2. *Why was it such a wonderful place?*
3. *What special person is at your church?*

WHAT DO YOU SEE?
Find the big bowl. Priests washed in it. It was a way to keep clean for God. Do you see the sacrifice burning? That was a way people told God they were sorry for their sins.

Our Church

Growing God's Way: We like to go to God's house together as a family.

You can see that this family looks happy. But what special building is that? Is it the grocery store? Is it the zoo? These people like to go to church. They like to read their Bibles in church. Do you suppose that's why they have their Bibles with them? Can you think of other things they will do today in church?

A TIME TO SHARE
1. *Where are these people going?*
2. *Why do they look glad to go here?*
3. *What do you learn at church and Sunday School?*

WHAT DO YOU SEE?
What do you see that tells you this is a church? How many Bibles do you see? Point to each of them.

Someone Loves Me

Growing God's Way: God gives us special people, like grandfathers and grandmothers, to love us.

Look at that boy rocking in the big chair. Who do you think usually sits there? Do you suppose that is Grandfather's chair? The boy likes to sit in Grandfather's chair. He sometimes likes to sit on Grandfather's lap and listen to a favorite Bible story. He knows Grandfather loves him. And he knows Jesus loves him too. That's what Grandfather's Bible story tells him.

A TIME TO SHARE
1. *Whose chair is this?*
2. *Why does the boy like to sit here?*
3. *Who loves this boy?*

WHAT DO YOU SEE?
Point to each thing you see at Grandfather's house. Which of these do you have at your house?

Helpers

Growing God's Way: God gives us fathers and mothers to help us.

Here's Father, trying to fix his boy's bike. And there's his boy, trying to help Father. Father is glad that he can help this way. The boy is glad he can help too. Do you think Jesus is pleased when we help each other?

WHAT DO YOU SEE?
What two tools do you see? What will Father do with each of these two tools? What other tools do you think you could find in the chest?

A TIME TO SHARE
1. *How is Father helping his boy?*
2. *How is the boy helping Father?*
3. *Why do you think this pleases Jesus?*

Jesus' Friends in Other Places

Growing God's Way: God wants us to love boys and girls in other places.

Look at those boys and girls in the picture on the wall. Where do you think each lives? Jesus loves boys and girls everywhere, doesn't He? He has friends over all the world. Does your church help Jesus' friends in other parts of the world?

A TIME TO SHARE
1. *Who does Jesus love?*
2. *Who did He die for?*
3. *Why should we be friends with Jesus' friends?*

WHAT DO YOU SEE?
What do the two boys have there? Why do you think they are looking at this globe of the world?

Wonderful Things to Eat

Growing God's Way: God gives many wonderful kinds of food to eat.

Have you ever seen such a big bunch of grapes? These men had never seen one that big. They are taking it back to show it to their friends. Do you think they had fun eating these beautiful grapes? You would, wouldn't you? Whenever you eat wonderful things like this, remember to thank God. They would never grow without His help.

WHAT DO YOU SEE?
How are these men carrying the grapes? Why are they carrying them with a pole? Why aren't these men dressed in jeans or a suit?

A TIME TO SHARE
1. What do these men have?
2. What will they do with these grapes?
3. How did God help them have the grapes?

Can You Make Yourself Well?

Growing God's Way: We are glad for bandages to help us when we are hurt.

What do you think happened to this boy? Mother is putting something on his finger. Do you know what it is? You've had bandages like this put on your finger, haven't you? But do you know how your finger gets well? Mother can't make your finger get well. Father can't do it. You can't do it. But God can. You must help Him by using medicine and bandages. But only God can make you well.

WHAT DO YOU SEE?
What do you see on the boy's face that tells you he is hurt? Point to the bandage. How will this help the boy get well?

A TIME TO SHARE
1. *What do you think the boy is saying to Mother?*
2. *What do you think Mother is saying to the boy?*

Mother's Helper

Growing God's Way: We learn to be good helpers as we grow up.

This girl is a good helper, isn't she? Do you think Mother is glad? But Mother is doing something special for the girl too. What would the girl do if Mother did not go to the grocery store? What would she do if Mother did not cook for her? Isn't it fun to help each other? Jesus wants us to do that and to help Him. How can you help Him? By doing what He tells you in the Bible. Can you think of some things? Are you glad you can be His helper?

A TIME TO SHARE
1. *How is the girl helping Mother?*
2. *How is Mother helping the girl?*
3. *How can Mother and the girl help Jesus?*

WHAT DO YOU SEE?
What kind of store is this? What do you see that tells you? What would you not see at a shoe store? Why not?

God Gives Us Many Good Things

Growing God's Way: God gives us food in many places.

Ummmm! Today this boy would rather have a hot dog than a steak. There is something about a hot dog when you are at the park. Or when you are at the zoo. And there's a special time for popcorn. But you wouldn't want popcorn for breakfast, would you? Or you wouldn't want breakfast cereal at the zoo. God gives us many good things. He helps us get the right food in many different places. He is a very wise God, isn't He?

A TIME TO SHARE
1. *What are Father and the boy eating?*
2. *Where do you like to eat hot dogs?*
3. *Are you glad God gave you many kinds of good food? Why?*

WHAT DO YOU SEE?
What do you think is on the hot dog? Point to the catsup. Which do you think is the mustard? Where do you think the pickle relish is? Where are the buns?

Who Sends Rainbows?
Growing God's Way: God gives us many beautiful things to see.

There is something beautiful in the sky! When did you last see a rainbow? This girl sees the beautiful rainbow. She wants her friends to see it too. Do you suppose she is telling them about God's promises? Noah learned that God always keeps His promises. God sent a rainbow to help him remember that. The next time you see a rainbow, remember God's promises.

WHAT DO YOU SEE?
What are these friends wearing? Do you think it was raining or snowing today? How do you know?

A TIME TO SHARE
1. What is that in the sky?
2. How does it help you remember God?
3. *How does it help you think about His promises?*

How God Talks to Us

Growing God's Way: God has special ways to talk to us.

Here's something you have never seen before. The bush is burning. But it never burns up. Moses had never seen anything like this. But he had never heard God talk to him before either. Usually God does not talk to us so we can hear Him. We can read what God says in the Bible. He helped some men write what He wants us to know. But on this day Moses could hear God's voice. So this was a special day for Moses. Would you like to have been there?

A TIME TO SHARE
1. *How is God talking to Moses here?*
2. *How does God talk to us today?*
3. *Do you like to talk to God? How?*
4. *Would you like to talk to Him now?*

WHAT DO YOU SEE?
Where is Moses? Point to him. How are his clothes different from your father's clothes? How is this bush different from the bushes in your yard?

Something Wonderful Up There

Growing God's Way: God made a beautiful moon to give us light at night.

Do you like to look up in the sky at night? What do you see? This boy sees something special. Last night Mother read a Bible story to this boy. He heard that God made the moon and put it in the sky. God made many other wonderful things and put them in the sky. Can you name some? The next time you see the moon, thank God for making it.

WHAT DO YOU SEE?
What time of day is this? How do you know? Why isn't it noon? What do you think Mother is doing now?

A TIME TO SHARE
1. *What does this boy see in the sky?*
2. *When did you last see the moon?*
3. *Who made the moon?*
4. *Would you like to thank God for it?*

Who Gives Good Food to Eat?

Growing God's Way: God gives us good food so we can grow strong.

Look who's having dinner tonight in the barn. Point to each animal that will eat something. This boy and girl are glad Grandfather lets them come to the barn. They can see that God gives good food to His animal friends. They also know that God gives good food to them too. Are you glad that God does this for you?

A TIME TO SHARE
1. *Who is feeding these animals?*
2. *Who caused this food to grow?*
3. *How does God give you good food?*

WHAT DO YOU SEE?
Can you find the food for the animals? Point to it. How many chickens do you see? Which one is the mother?

God Helps Me Taste Good Things

Growing God's Way: We are glad that God helps us taste good things.

Here is a store that sells ice cream. You may buy it in dishes, or in cones. You may choose your favorite flavor. What would you like today? Do you want chocolate, or vanilla, or strawberry? You can see that this boy has two of his favorite flavors. What do you think they are? Aren't you glad that God helps you taste all these wonderful flavors?

WHAT DO YOU SEE?
Is this a summer day or a winter day? How do you know? Point to four ways you can buy your ice cream.

A TIME TO SHARE
1. *Which flavors of ice cream do you think you could buy here?*
2. *Which flavors do you like best?*
3. *Who helps you taste these flavors?*

Buying a Red Balloon

Growing God's Way: God helps us see many beautiful colors.

Look at all those beautiful balloons. They are not all the same color, are they? This boy wants to buy one, and it will be his favorite color. Which balloon do you think he will buy? Which one would you like to buy?

A TIME TO SHARE
1. Who will pay for the boy's balloon?
2. How do you know?
3. What should the boy say?
4. What is the other boy doing? Why?

WHAT DO YOU SEE?
How many colors do you see? Do you have some crayons? How many colors do you have? Are you glad God lets you see all these colors? Be sure to thank Him.

Doing What God Wants

Growing God's Way: God wants us to learn to obey Him.

Have you ever heard a donkey talk? Balaam had never heard a donkey talk either. Then suddenly his donkey told him something. Actually God was making the donkey talk. He told Balaam that God wanted him to obey. Balaam listened. Then Balaam obeyed God. God wants us to obey Him too, doesn't He?

WHAT DO YOU SEE?
What kind of animal is Balaam riding? What does Balaam have in his left hand? What do you think he does with it? What is in his other hand? What does he do with that?

A TIME TO SHARE
1. Who talked with Balaam?
2. What did he tell Balaam?
3. Why should you obey God?

WHAT DO YOU SEE?
How many birds do you see? How many of them are flying? What is the bird in the tree doing?

Look at the Birds

Growing God's Way: God teaches birds special things. We may learn special things from Him too.

Look at those birds! That cat is looking at them. He would like to catch one. But he won't. The birds will fly away. But who teaches them to fly? Have you ever tried to teach a bird to fly? Do you think you could? Only God can do that. It is only one of the wonderful things that God teaches His animal friends. He will teach you many wonderful things too. Will you let Him?

A TIME TO SHARE
1. *Who teaches birds to fly?*
2. *Why can't you do that?*
3. *What special things can you learn from God? Will you?*

A Quiet Place

Growing God's Way: God made many wonderful things for us to see.

Do you like to go camping? This family does. They like to drive to a quiet place and put up their tent. They like to talk by a crackling campfire. What do you think they are saying? Do you think they will talk about God? Do you think they are glad for the wonderful things God made?

WHAT DO YOU SEE?
Point to some things you do not usually see on a city street. Is this daytime or nighttime? How do you know?

A TIME TO SHARE
1. *What do you see that God has made?*
2. *What do you see that people made?*
3. *Do you like to go camping? Why?*
4. *What would you like to do here?*

Special Food in Summer

Growing God's Way: God gives us special food in summer.

Now here is something you don't do when the snow is blowing. In most parts of the country, watermelons grow only in the summer. So do many other special foods. These are special summer treats for most of us. "Come and get it," Father says. Would you like to have a piece of this special summer food? Be sure to thank Father for it. And be sure to thank God too.

A TIME TO SHARE
1. *What is this special food?*
2. *Does it grow in the winter in your part of the country? Why not?*
3. *Be sure to thank God for special food.*

WHAT DO YOU SEE?
Where is this family eating? Is it in their dining room? How many pieces of watermelon has Father cut? What do you think Mother is bringing?

I'll Catch You!

Growing God's Way: Father or Mother won't let us fall, and neither will God.

Do you like to go on a slide? Do you remember when you were little? You were afraid to do it. But Father or Mother was there to catch you. "I'll catch you," Father or Mother said. "I won't let you fall." Did they? Of course not. God will be there to help you too. Why not ask Him?

A TIME TO SHARE
1. What is the boy doing? What will the girl do?
2. Who is there to catch them?
3. Do you think this boy or girl will get hurt? Why not? Who else will take care of them?

WHAT DO YOU SEE?
How many steps do you see on the slide? Who is helping the boy and girl get up? Who is helping catch them?

A Place that Is Safe

Growing God's Way: When storms or troubles come, we need a safe place.

Look! Do you see those ponies running? They know a storm is coming. Father knows it too. "Hurry!" he says to the ponies. The boy is also telling the ponies to hurry. They want a safe place during the storm. Do you think they saw the lightning? Do you think they heard the thunder? The boy heard the thunder too, but he feels safe with his father. Do you feel safe when you are with Mother or Father? Do you feel safe when you know God is with you?

A TIME TO SHARE
1. *Why isn't the boy afraid? Who is with him? Why isn't Father afraid? Who is with him?*
2. *Who is with you during a storm? Who is with you when you have trouble?*

WHAT DO YOU SEE?
How do you know that a storm is coming? Point to three things that tell you.

God Gives Us Clouds

Growing God's Way: We should thank God for special gifts, like clouds.

This girl and her father are having a wonderful time. Do you like to hike with Mother or Father? You see many beautiful things on a hike, don't you? This girl is pointing to the puffy white clouds. Some look like elephants, or lions, or alligators. Some look like faces. Father and the girl are talking about the clouds. They talk about the fun things they see in the clouds. And they talk about the way God made this beautiful world. They are glad for the beautiful clouds. Are you?

WHAT DO YOU SEE?
Are Father and the girl on a city street? Where are they? Point to some things that tell you this is out in the country.

A TIME TO SHARE
1. *How many clouds do you see?*
2. *Why does God send the clouds? What does He do with them?*
3. *Would you like to thank God for the clouds?*

The People Here Will Be Safe

Growing God's Way: God keeps us safe when we obey Him.

This is Rahab's house. It is different from your house. Rahab's house is built on a city wall. It is not made of wood and plaster, with glass windows, like yours. But Rahab liked her house. It kept her safe. One day two men came to Rahab's house. They were spies. Somehow Rahab knew that their people, the Israelites, would capture her city. She would not be safe in her house then. "I will help you if you will help me," Rahab told the spies. Then Rahab helped the men escape from the city. "Keep this scarlet cord in your window," the spies told her. "As long as it is there, you will be safe. Our people will not hurt you." Of course Rahab kept the scarlet cord in her window.

A TIME TO SHARE
1. Who did Rahab help? How? Who helped Rahab? How?
2. What would have happened to Rahab if she had not done what the men said? Why is it important to obey?

WHAT DO YOU SEE?
How is Rahab's house different from your house? What do you see in her window? Why is the scarlet cord there?

Something Good to Drink

Growing God's Way: God gives us good things to drink when we are thirsty.

When was the last time you were hot and thirsty? What did you want? This boy wants a glass of Mother's cold lemonade. Do you think he will get it? Mother knows he is thirsty. That is why she made the lemonade. She squeezed juice from some lemons. God made the lemons grow on trees. Then Mother added water. God gives us good water to drink. How could we ever have cold lemonade without God's wonderful gifts. He gives us many good things to drink when we are thirsty.

WHAT DO YOU SEE?
What did Mother use to make this lemonade? Point to each thing and tell what it is. Where is the lemon? Where is the sugar? Where did the water come from?

A TIME TO SHARE
1. What two things does Mother have?
2. What was the boy doing that made him thirsty?
3. What should the boy say to Mother now? What should he say to God now?

What Do You Put in Your Pockets?

Growing God's Way: God gives us clothing to wear.

Do you have pockets in the clothes you are wearing? Look at what you have on. How many pockets do you have? What do you have in them? This boy has found something in his pocket. What is it? What do you think Father has in his pockets? What do you think Mother has in her pockets? God gives us clothing to wear. Aren't you glad He does? And aren't you glad for pockets in your clothes?

A TIME TO SHARE
1. Can you name each kind of clothing that you have? Are you glad for each one?
2. Have you thanked God for each?
3. Thank God for pockets too. They are fun, and help you carry things you need.

WHAT DO YOU SEE?
How many pockets can you count? Point to each one. What do you think each person puts in those pockets?

What Are They Eating?

Growing God's Way: God gives each of His creatures a special kind of food.

Do you see what I see? It's like a little ocean or lake with glass walls. This girl likes her aquarium. She likes to feed the goldfish in it. But look at the food she is giving her goldfish. It does not look at all like the food her brother is giving Kitty. Do you suppose Kitty would like the goldfish food? Do you suppose the goldfish would like Kitty's food? Why not? You wouldn't want to eat either food, would you? That's the way God planned it. He made a special kind of food for each of his creatures. God knows what is best for us, doesn't He?

A TIME TO SHARE
1. *What kind of food do you see here?*
2. *What kinds of foods do you eat?*
3. *Name some foods for other creatures.*
4. *Do you thank God for your food?*

WHAT DO YOU SEE?
How many goldfish do you see? Why don't they get on the floor and eat from Kitty's dish? How many cats do you see? Why doesn't Kitty swim in the aquarium and eat the goldfish food? God does all things the right way, doesn't He?

Do You Like to Play?

Growing God's Way: God gives us playtime as part of our growing-up time.

Look at Puppy run! You can see that he is having fun. You can see that the boy and girl are having fun too. Playtime is fun time. How would you like to grow up without any playtime? God would not want you to do that. You would not be a fun person. God made us so we want to play. Playtime is part of God's growing-up time for us. Let's thank God for playtime now.

A TIME TO SHARE
1. What are the boy and girl doing?
2. Who is having fun?
3. What do you do to have fun?
4. Why does God give us playtime?

WHAT DO YOU SEE?
Whose room is this? How do you know? Point to some things that tell you this is a boy's room.

Follow Me!

Growing God's Way: God wants us to learn to follow Him.

Do you play a trumpet? If you do, it certainly is not like this one. Gideon did not play his trumpet in a band or orchestra. He did not play it in a school program. Gideon blew his trumpet so his soldiers would hear it. That was his way of saying, "Follow me!" Then Gideon led his soldiers into a battle. The soldiers would not win the battle if they did not obey and follow Gideon. God wants us to learn to follow Him. He won't blow a trumpet, but He does tell us in the Bible how to follow Him.

WHAT DO YOU SEE?
Where is Gideon? Point to his trumpet. It is made from an animal horn. Do you think Gideon is blowing on it now?

A TIME TO SHARE
1. *Why did Gideon blow on his trumpet? What was he saying to his soldiers?*
2. *Where does God tell us how to follow Him? Would you like to follow Him?*

Who Made the Pond?

Growing God's Way: When we see a pond, we should think about God.

Do you like to visit a little pond? This boy and girl have a pond near their house. It is a favorite place to go. "Look!" the boy says. "Do you see the big frog?" The girl sees it. "Look!" says the girl. "Do you see the cattails?" The boy sees them. What else do you see in this pond? Can you find anything here that God did not make? When you see a pond, think about God.

WHAT DO YOU SEE?
Point to four things that tell you this is a pond. Can you name each of these? Why would these four things not grow in your living room?

A TIME TO SHARE
1. *What is sitting on the rock? What is swimming on the water?*
2. *Why doesn't a frog say "quack"? Why don't ducks say "gerunk"?*
3. *Are you glad God made each thing for a special place? Say "thank You, God."*

89

Good Morning, Merry Sunshine!

Growing God's Way: God wants us to be thankful for each new day.

Good morning, merry sunshine! It is time to get up. The sun is shining, and God has given us a new day. The boy has many fun things to do today. He wants to go outside and play. The sunshine feels warm and friendly on his face. This is a new day. God has given it to us. It is different from yesterday. It will be different from tomorrow. Would you like to thank God for today?

WHAT DO YOU SEE?
How do you know this is morning? Point to some things that tell you it is not noon or night.

A TIME TO SHARE
1. *What does the boy see outside?*
2. *Are you thankful for each day?*
3. *Will you thank God for giving you today?*

A Special Time with Father or Mother

Growing God's Way: God gives fathers and mothers to help us grow God's way.

Oh, what a wonderful day for a walk! What a wonderful day to sit in the grass and talk! Today this boy is walking with Father. Tomorrow he may go for a walk with Mother. You can see that Father and the boy are having fun together. Do you like to do things with Mother or Father? Do you like to talk about special things you see? Why do you think God gives us mothers and fathers?

A TIME TO SHARE
1. What are Father and the boy doing?
2. Would you like to do this with your father or mother?
3. What would you say if you were here?

WHAT DO YOU SEE?
How do you know this is in the country? Point to some things you would not see on a city street. Is this winter or summer? How do you know?

91

Some Things Are Cold

Growing God's Way: We should be thankful for things that are cold or hot.

Here's something you would do on a summer day. You wouldn't want ice cream to eat while you are building a snowman. And you wouldn't want a cup of hot chocolate on a hot summer afternoon. That's the time for cold lemonade. Aren't you glad that some food or drink is good when it is hot? And other food or drink is better when it is cold. God had a wonderful plan when He gave us hot and cold, didn't He? Don't forget that other things are better when they are just warm. So be sure to thank God for cold or hot, or just warm.

A TIME TO SHARE
1. Why would you like a cold drink on a hot summer day? Why not a hot drink?
2. Would you like to take a bath in ice-cold water? Why not? Aren't you glad God gives us cold and hot, and just warm?

WHAT DO YOU SEE?
Is this a summer day or a winter day? How do you know? Point to the ice cubes. Will they make the lemonade cold or hot?

Will You Show Me How?

***Growing God's Way:** Mothers and fathers help us grow God's way by showing us how to do things.*

This looks like fun. But how do you do it? Father will show the boy how. Do you think the boy is glad that Father is there? Fathers and mothers show boys and girls how to do many good things. Boys and girls grow best when mothers and fathers show them how to do things. Are you glad they do? What does your father or mother help you do?

A TIME TO SHARE
1. *What is the boy trying to do?*
2. *Why is Father there?*
3. *What has your father or mother helped you do today? Did you thank them?*

WHAT DO YOU SEE?
What is the boy holding in his hand? Point to the arrow. Where will the arrow go when Father shows him what to do?

WHAT DO YOU SEE?
Where did this feather come from? How many geese do you see? Do you think Father and the girl will feed the geese? Where do you think the feed is now?

Special Clothes for Animal Friends

Growing God's Way: God gives animal friends special clothes to wear.

Look what this girl found! The geese do not mind. This was an extra feather that one of them did not need. The goose dropped the feather on the ground. But geese do need most of their feathers. Feathers are like clothing to the geese. Geese could not fly or swim without their feathers. They could not keep warm either. God makes special clothing for each kind of animal friend. Don't you think geese are glad they don't have wool? And sheep would look strange with feathers. God gave the right kind of clothing to each one.

A TIME TO SHARE
1. What did the girl find?
2. Why did God give feathers to geese?
3. *What are some other kinds of animal clothing?*

Taking Care of the Sheep

***Growing God's Way:** A shepherd takes care of his sheep, and God takes care of us.*

That lion had better watch out! If it tries to hurt David's sheep, it is in trouble. David is a shepherd. He will take care of his sheep. He will even fight a lion to do this. Aren't you glad to see a shepherd take care of his sheep? Aren't you glad God takes care of you?

WHAT DO YOU SEE?
Where is the lion? What does the lion want to do? Point to David's sling. What will he do with the rock in it?

A TIME TO SHARE
1. *What will David do with his sling?*
2. *How does his sling help take care of his sheep?*
3. *How does God take care of you?*

What Is God Doing at Dandelion Hill?

Growing God's Way: *We learn to be thankful when we see special things God has made.*

Do you think this family is having fun on Dandelion Hill? You can see that they are. This is their favorite picnic spot. But why do you think they call this Dandelion Hill? "Look!" says the girl. "Watch!" says the boy. Mother and Father watch the boy and girl have fun with dandelions. Do you like to blow the puffy white balls? Do you see the little seeds float in the air? God made this special way for the dandelion seeds to travel to other places where they will grow.

Dandelion Hill reminds this family that God has special ways to take care of His plants. He also has special ways to take care of His people.

A TIME TO SHARE
1. *What is this family doing?*
2. *Why do you think they are having fun?*
3. *How does God help dandelion seeds get to other places where they will grow? How does He help other seeds do this?*

WHAT DO YOU SEE?
What color are dandelions when you can blow them to the wind? What color are they before you can do this? Point to some dandelions on Dandelion Hill.

Mother and Father Are with Me

Growing God's Way: We are glad when Mother or Father is with us.

Do you see where this girl is riding? A merry-go-round is a special place. You can pretend that you are riding away to some exciting place. Around and around you go. But each time you come back, you are so glad to see Mother or Father waving to you. When your ride is over, Mother or Father will be there to talk about it. God gives us mothers and fathers to take care of us. Aren't you glad Mother or Father is there when you need them?

A TIME TO SHARE
1. *What is the girl riding on?*
2. *Where do you think she is going?*
3. *Who is there to wave to her?*
4. *Have you thanked God for Mother or Father today? Will you?*

WHAT DO YOU SEE?
Where is the girl's mother? Where is her father? Where is her little brother? Why do you think he isn't on the merry-go-round? What does Father have in his hand?

God Takes Care of the Birds

Growing God's Way: God helps a woodpecker find food.

Listen! Do you hear what I hear? Do you hear that noise up in the tree? There it is! These girls and the boy have found it. Now do you see what they see? Why do you think the woodpecker is pecking on the tree? It's fun to watch it work. It pecks a hole to find things to eat. Sometimes it pecks a big hole for its home. A robin doesn't make a home or store its food this way. Most other birds don't either. But that's the way God made the woodpecker. Let's thank God for sending woodpeckers for us to see.

A TIME TO SHARE
1. *What is the woodpecker doing?*
2. *Why does he do things this way?*
3. *Are you glad to see birds in your backyard? Be sure to thank God for them.*

WHAT DO YOU SEE?
Point to the woodpecker. What part of it hits the tree? What part of the bird holds onto the tree? What part helps the bird fly?

What Would We Do without Grass?

Growing God's Way: God gives us grass to help us in many ways. We should be thankful that He does.

Do you like to roll in the grass on a beautiful day? These boys do. You can see they are having fun. It would not be much fun to roll in gravel or mud, would it? Father likes grass too. He likes to mow the grass and make the lawn look neat. Something else in this picture likes grass. Do you see it? What is the cow doing with the grass?

A TIME TO SHARE
1. *Why do the boys like the grass?*
2. *Why does Father like the grass?*
3. *Why does the cow like the grass?*
4. *Why should you thank God for grass?*

WHAT DO YOU SEE?
Is this in town or in the country? How do you know? Point to some places where you see grass. Point to some places where you do not see grass. Who made the grass?

God Gives Us Food to Eat

Growing God's Way: God gives us good food to help us grow.

Elijah is a hungry man. But where will he get food to eat? There are no grocery stores. There are no crops because there is no rain. Everyone else in the land is hungry too. There is no food to eat. But God has some food for Elijah. He is giving it to Elijah in a special way. Do you see how God is sending the food to Elijah?

A TIME TO SHARE
1. *What are the birds bringing Elijah?*
2. *Why doesn't Elijah buy food at the grocery store?*
3. *Who sent these birds with food?*
4. *What should Elijah say to God? Why?*

WHAT DO YOU SEE?
How many birds do you see? These birds are called ravens. Which bird is giving Elijah food to eat? Point to the food. Point to the three ravens.

Doing Things Together

Growing God's Way: *We grow God's way with good friends to help us.*

If you've ever had a tree house, you know how much fun it can be. But it is not much fun if you are alone. These boys are having fun in their tree house. But that's because they are doing things together. What are some special things you like to do with your friends? Where are some special places you like to play with them? We should thank God for giving us good friends. Growing God's way is growing up with God's friends.

A TIME TO SHARE
1. *How do you know these boys are friends? How do you know they are having fun together?*
2. *Who are your good friends? Do you have friends who help you love God? Do you help your friends love God?*

WHAT DO YOU SEE?
What kind of house is this? How do these friends get up in it? Why do they have to be careful when they are playing there?

Do You Like Cool Water?

***Growing God's Way:** What would we do without cool water? God knew this so He gives us cool water for many things.*

Now this looks like fun on a hot summer day. Who doesn't like cool running water at a time like this? Do you? These boys have been playing in the park on a hot day. Now they are glad for cool water. Sometimes we like cool water to drink. At other times we like to splash our feet in it, or go swimming. God gives us cool water for many things. What would we do without it?

WHAT DO YOU SEE?
Is this a drinking fountain? Is it a fire hydrant? What is this? Why do you think this is in town? Is it summer or winter? How do you know?

A TIME TO SHARE
1. *What are the boys doing? Could they do this without water? Why not?*
2. *What are some things you like to do with cool water?*
3. *Have you thanked God today for cool water?*

God Made Many Kinds of Animals

Growing God's Way: God made many kinds of animals for us to enjoy.

Do you like to visit a zoo? This family does. You can see how much fun they are having. Would you like to watch this animal eat? What kind of animal is it? You would not want to take it home for a pet, would you? Why do you think Mother or Father would not like this animal for a pet? God made many kinds of animals for us to enjoy. Animals do many good things for us.

A TIME TO SHARE
1. *How is the elephant eating? Why doesn't he use his hands?*
2. *Why wouldn't the elephant make a good pet in your house?*

WHAT DO YOU SEE?
Is the elephant bigger or smaller than the boy and girl? Why is it better for the elephant to live in a zoo or in the jungle than at your house?

I Like My Mother's Face

Growing God's Way: God planned for our faces to say many things to those around us.

Do you like to look at your mother's face? This girl does. Sometimes Mother's face smiles at the girl. That makes the girl feel warm and happy inside. Sometimes the girl does something that does not please Mother. When Mother frowns, the girl knows that something is not right. Mother's face changes many times each day. Sometimes her eyes twinkle and her lips look soft and warm. When that happens, Mother's face reminds the girl of a sunshiny day. Our faces say many things, don't they? Do you ever look in the mirror to see what your face is saying? Does your face tell others, "God loves you?"

WHAT DO YOU SEE?
Point to Mother's eyes. Where are her lips? When Mother smiles, how do each of these change? Look in the mirror. Do you like to smile? What does your smile say to others?

A TIME TO SHARE
1. *Who is with this girl?*
2. *Is Mother happy or sad? How do you know? Is the girl happy or sad?*
3. *Why do you think Jesus is happy when Mother and her girl are like this?*

Building Something Special

Growing God's Way: It's fun to build something special when we know God wants us to do it.

Look at all those big stones! Would you use them to build a tree house? Would you use them to build a dog house? Of course not! They are too big, aren't they? But Nehemiah was using them. He and his friends were building a big wall around Jerusalem. Nehemiah was sure God wanted him to do this. That's a good reason to build something special, isn't it?

WHAT DO YOU SEE?
How many men do you see? What is each man doing? What would you say to these men if you were here?

A TIME TO SHARE
1. What are Nehemiah and his friends doing with these big stones?
2. Why do you think they want to do this? Who wants them to do it?
3. What are some things God wants you to do? Do you like to do these things?

I Smell Something Good

Growing God's Way: God gave us noses so we can smell good things.

This boy smelled something good this morning when he woke up. It didn't take long for him to get dressed. He likes to eat pancakes. Do you? Mother dips up some pancake batter and plops it into the frying pan. Before long the boy will turn the pancake over. It will be a toasty brown. You can almost smell that wonderful pancake cooking, can't you?

WHAT DO YOU SEE?
How many noses do you see here? How many noses smell the pancake? Point to each thing that Mother used to make the pancake. Can you name each one?

A TIME TO SHARE
1. What is Mother making?
2. Do pancakes smell good or bad?
3. Name some things that smell good. Let's thank God for a nose to smell good things.

Do You Like Clean Clothes?

***Growing God's Way:** God wants us to be neat and clean, so we should do our best to help Mother or Father keep us clean.*

Do your clothes ever get dirty? Do they wash themselves? This girl gets her clothes dirty. That's because she likes to play and clothes do get dirty that way. But her clothes will not wash themselves. Yours won't either. Mother has just washed this girl's clothes. She is hanging them out to dry. You can see how much fun it is for the girl to help her. But you can also see that the girl could not do all of this herself. Do you think she is glad that Mother does this for her? Do you think she is glad she can help Mother keep her clothes clean?

A TIME TO SHARE
1. *Why is the girl happy? Why is Mother happy?*
2. *Are you glad when Mother washes your clothes? Are you glad when you can help her? Be sure to help Mother when she is trying to help you.*

WHAT DO YOU SEE?
What is Mother hanging on the line? What is she holding in her hands? What is the girl carrying? Why does Mother need these?

Someone to Play with Me

Growing God's Way: God knows we should not grow up alone, so He gives us someone special to play with us.

Do you have a favorite swing somewhere? Is it in your backyard? Or is it at Grandfather's or Grandmother's house? This girl has a favorite swing. She also has someone to help her swing. Up and back, up and back. Father pushes the girl and the wind whispers on her face as she swings. Are you glad when someone special helps you swing? This girl is. God knows you need someone special to play with you. Are you glad when Mother or Father can do that? Are you glad when Grandmother or Grandfather can do it?

WHAT DO YOU SEE?
What holds the swing up? Do you suppose Father checked the ropes to make sure they were strong enough? What else do you see in the picture?

A TIME TO SHARE
1. *Who is helping this girl swing?*
2. *Why is it more fun when someone plays with us?*
3. *What special things do you like to do with Mother or Father?*

Do You Like to Be Brave?

Growing God's Way: God wants us to learn to be brave.

Do you ever sleep in a tent in your backyard? This is the first time this boy has done it. Father thinks he is a brave boy. Of course he does have Puppy to stay with him. And he is glad for his flashlight too. But something said WHOOOOOO. The boy didn't feel very brave then. But now the boy feels brave again. Father is there to check up on him. Everything will be all right now; don't you think so?

A TIME TO SHARE

1. *How do you think the boy felt when something went WHOOOOOO? How do you think he felt when Father came?*
2. *Why does God want us to learn to be brave? He is with us at all times, so we should ask Him to help us be brave.*

WHAT DO YOU SEE?
Point to something that made the boy afraid. Point to some things that helped the boy be brave.

A Special Book

Growing God's Way: God gave us a special Book, the Bible, to help us grow His way.

This man is reading a Book. It doesn't look much like your favorite book, does it? But this was the way people made books in Bible times. These books were called scrolls. Someone had to write every word on it. There was no other way to do it. They did not have printing presses yet. But this Book was God's Word, just as your Bible is God's Word. Aren't you glad God gives His Word to help us grow the way He wants?

A TIME TO SHARE
1. *What is this man reading?*
2. *Why is he glad to read it?*
3. *What will God's Word help you do?*

WHAT DO YOU SEE?
Point to the two ends of the scroll. Do you see how the paper rolls up on each end? How many hands does this man need to hold the scroll? Why?

My Special Book

Growing God's Way: God wants us to read His Book, the Bible, so that we will grow His way.

This boy likes to read. You can see that. Look at all the books on his shelf. But he is reading his favorite Book now. This is a Book that God wrote. Do you know what it is? Mother and Father gave this Bible to the boy. That makes this Bible even more special. Do you like to read your Bible? God is pleased when you do.

A TIME TO SHARE

1. What is the boy doing? Which Book is he reading?
2. What do you think the boy will learn?
3. Why do you read your Bible? What will it help you do?

WHAT DO YOU SEE?
How do you know this is a boy's room? Point to some things that tell you this is not the kitchen. Why do you think the boy likes to read his Bible?

Working Together as a Family

Growing God's Way: God wants us to have fun when we work together as a family.

Look at this busy family. Each person is doing something special. Do you see anyone sitting there, watching the others work? This family likes to do things together. Mother is busy. Father is doing his part. And the boy and girl are having fun because they like to help Mother and Father. They laugh and talk about fun things while they wash the dishes. When the dishes are done, this family will play a game together. Sometime this evening they will read the Bible and pray together. Don't you think God is pleased when He sees this family doing things together?

WHAT DO YOU SEE?
What is Father doing? What is Mother doing? What are the boy and girl doing? How many dishes can you count?

A TIME TO SHARE
1. Why do you think the boy and girl are happy?
2. Why wouldn't this family look as happy if Mother were doing all the work?
3. Why is God pleased to see a family working together like this?

Playtime Is Growing Time

Growing God's Way: God plans for us to play as well as work.

This boy and girl are not doing their chores right now. That's because they already did them. And they did their homework too. Now it's time to play. Puppy and Kitty want to play too. "Will you come into my castle?" the boy asks. It's really nothing but a big box, isn't it? But the boy and girl can pretend that it is anything. Aren't you glad God planned for us to play? It would be no fun to work all the time, would it?

WHAT DO YOU SEE?
Who is playing in this box? Think of some things that could have been in this box when it came to them. This boy and girl are pretending the box is a castle. What would you pretend it is?

A TIME TO SHARE
1. What did you do when you played this week? What did you do when you worked this week? God wants us to do both, doesn't He?
2. Why do you think God wants us to play?

What Would We Do Without Music?

Growing God's Way: God made it possible for us to have many kinds of music.

Do you play in a band or orchestra? Do you sing or play the piano? It's fun to play music, isn't it? You can see that these people are having fun playing their instruments. And Father is having fun with his family listening to them. God planned for music. Music is one of the wonderful gifts that He has given. Would you like to play or sing for God?

WHAT DO YOU SEE?
How many musical instruments do you see? Can you name each one? How many other musical instruments can you name?

A TIME TO SHARE
1. Why are the people in the band having fun? Why are Father and his family having fun?
2. Do you sing songs at church and Sunday School? How many instruments are played there? Ask what kind of music you could play or sing to praise God.

A Way to Earn a Living

Growing God's Way: God planned for each of us to find a special way to earn our living.

What does your father or mother do to earn a living? Do they work in an office? Do they wear uniforms? This man does not work in an office. He does not wear a uniform. But he is earning a living. He catches fish with those big nets and sells them. Sometimes the man's nets tear and he must fix them. Do you think he is doing that now? God helps firemen, and policemen, and farmers, and nurses, and many others to earn a living. And he helps fishermen like this to earn a living too.

A TIME TO SHARE
1. *How does this man earn a living?*
2. *Why is it important for each person to earn a living in some way?*
3. *Do you think Jesus saw men like this? What do you think He said to them?*

WHAT DO YOU SEE?
What is the man fixing? Which net is drying? These nets are the man's tools to help him earn a living. A carpenter has other tools. Can you name some of them? Can you name the tools other people use to earn a living?

God Made Animals Different from People

Growing God's Way: God made His animal friends, and us, to be different from others.

Look! What do you see? Are those elephants? Are they zebras? Are they horses? How do you know they are not these animals? How do you know they are giraffes? God made each kind of animal different from other kinds of animals. He also made you to be different from every other boy or girl on earth. That tells you how much He loves you, doesn't it? Think how you would feel if you were exactly like every other boy or girl in the world.

A TIME TO SHARE
1. Why is the giraffe different from an elephant or a horse? Why didn't God make all animals to be exactly alike?
2. Why are you different from all other boys and girls? Why didn't God make all boys and girls to be exactly alike?

WHAT DO YOU SEE?
Where are these animals? Is this a jungle? Is it a zoo? Point to some things you would not see at your home.

Doing Things Together

***Growing God's Way:** God is pleased when we do things together as a family.*

Where are these people today? Are they at the zoo? Are they in their backyard? They like to come to the beach together. Sometimes they swim. Sometimes they sit on the beach and talk. And sometimes they do other fun things. Can you name some of the fun things they are doing together today?

A TIME TO SHARE
1. *What is Mother doing? What are the boy and girl doing with Father?*
2. *Do you think they like to do things together? How do you know?*
3. *Why is Jesus pleased when families do things together?*

WHAT DO YOU SEE?
Point to some things that tell you this is the beach. What do you see that you would not see in your living room? How many birds can you find?

Grandfathers Are Special!

Growing God's Way: God gave us special people called grandfathers. We should do special things with them.

This girl is having a special day. That's because she is spending the day with a special person. Her grandfather does not live in the city. You can see that if you look closely at his backyard. Would you like to come with this girl today to her grandfather's house? If you did, you could pump water from Grandfather's old pump. You could do other fun things that people do in the country. Don't you think this girl is glad that God gave her a special grandfather? Don't you think she is thankful that she can do special things with him?

WHAT DO YOU SEE?
Who is getting a drink of water? Point to three friends. What is Grandfather doing? How do you know this is not in the city?

A TIME TO SHARE
1. Why are grandfathers special people?
2. What do you like to do with your grandfather? Why?
3. Would you like to call Grandfather or send a letter to him? Be sure to tell him how much you love him.

WHAT DO YOU SEE?
How do you know that this is not a windy day? Who has made the biggest bubble? Where is the smallest? Can you count all the bubbles?

Do You Like to Blow Bubbles?

Growing God's Way: God makes special shapes and special colors. You may see both in the bubbles you blow.

What a wonderful time to blow bubbles in your backyard! It's a summer afternoon and there is a soft breeze blowing. You can see that these boys and girls are having fun together as they blow bubbles. But look! These bubbles are not square. They are round. That's the way God makes bubbles. If you look closely at the bubbles you blow you will see many special colors in them. Sometimes they look like a rainbow spilled its colors on them. God makes things in many shapes and many colors. Aren't you glad God made bubbles to have different shapes and colors?

A TIME TO SHARE
1. *Do you like to blow bubbles? Why? Why is it more fun to do with friends?*
2. *What colors do you see in a bubble? What shape do you see? What are some other colors and shapes that God made?*

Someone New Is Here!

Growing God's Way: People and animals are born into this world. That's the way God planned it.

Someone new has come to Grandfather's farm. This little colt was not here yesterday. He was inside his mother. Now look at him. That's the way God planned for people and animals to come into the world. They grow inside their mothers until they are strong. When God knows they are ready, they are born. God has some wonderful plans, doesn't He?

WHAT DO YOU SEE?
How do you know this is a barn? What is Grandfather holding? Point to it. Do you have a flashlight or lantern? How is Grandfather's lantern different from yours?

A TIME TO SHARE
1. *Where was this colt yesterday? Where is he now? How did he get here?*
2. *How did you get here? Did you hatch from an egg or were you born also?*
3. *Let's thank God for His wonderful plans.*

Watching Seeds Grow

Growing God's Way: God planned for seeds to grow into strong plants that give us many things we need.

Do you see what this man is throwing onto the ground? He is not throwing those seeds away. He is planting them. God will send rain on the seeds. The warm sun will shine. One day some seeds will grow into beautiful green wheat plants. The plants will grow tall and more wheat seeds will grow on them. The farmer will harvest the wheat. He will keep some seeds to plant next year. But he will grind most of them into flour. Would you like to eat some of the fresh bread the farmer's wife will make from that wheat? God planned for seeds to grow into plants. We get many good things from plants.

A TIME TO SHARE
1. *What is the man throwing?*
2. *What will happen to most of the seeds?*
3. *How do we get food from these seeds, and the plants that grow from them?*
4. *Who planned for seeds to grow?*

WHAT DO YOU SEE?
Where is this man getting the seed? Point to the ground where the seed will grow. Point to the ground where the seed will not grow. Why not?

People Who Protect Us

Growing God's Way: We are glad for people who protect us. God also protects us each day.

Listen to that loud noise! Here comes the fire engine. Do you hear the siren whining? Do you see the red lights flashing? Do you hear the big motor roar as the fire engine whizzes by? But look, there's a friendly person on the fire engine. Do you see him waving? The boy does, and he is waving back. He knows the firemen are his friends. If his house caught on fire, the firemen would put it out. If his cat cannot get down from a high pole or tree, the firemen would help him get it down. The boy is thankful for his firemen friends. He knows God uses them to help protect him.

A TIME TO SHARE
1. *How do firemen help protect you and your family?*
2. *How does God protect you and your family?*
3. *Have you said "thank you" to your firemen friends? Have you said "thank You" to God?*

WHAT DO YOU SEE?
How do you know there is a fire? What do you see that tells you this? How many firemen do you see? Where is the hose they will use for the water?

Brothers and Sisters Are Fun

Growing God's Way: Sometimes God gives us a brother or sister. We are thankful for each other.

Do you have a brother or sister? If you do, you know how much fun that can be. Of course, brothers and sisters don't have fun every minute. Sometimes they argue or quarrel. But usually they are sorry about that. Before long they are having fun together. You can see how much fun this brother and sister are having together. Are you glad God gave you a brother or sister? If you are, thank Him right now!

A TIME TO SHARE
1. *Why should we be glad for brothers or sisters? Are you?*
2. *What are some special things your brother or sister has done for you? What are some special things you have done for them? Do you pray for each other?*

WHAT DO YOU SEE?
Where are this brother and sister? How do you know they are not in the living room? Point to some things that tell you this is the backyard. Who else is with them?

WHAT DO YOU SEE?
How do you know this is a pond? Why isn't it a desert? What do you see here that you would not see in your house? How many flying birds do you see?

Discovering Something New
Growing God's Way: God helps us find many new and wonderful things in His beautiful world.

Look what this boy has found! He would never see these ducks in his backyard. He would never see them on the streets of his city. But he has found them in this special place. That's because ducks like a pond, or lake, or river. God made them that way. What are some new and wonderful things you have seen in God's beautiful world this week?

A TIME TO SHARE
1. *How do you know that Father and the boy are having fun?*
2. *Why is it more fun to discover something new with someone you love instead of finding it by yourself?*
3. *Are you glad God made new surprises, like these ducks and cattails?*

Eating Can Be Fun!

Growing God's Way: *God gives us food to help us grow, but it is more fun to eat with others than to eat alone.*

Picnics are fun times, aren't they? That's because we like to get together with special friends. We talk and laugh, and sometimes play games. But a picnic would not be a picnic without good things to eat. Good food will help us grow. But God made us so that we can have fun eating good food. And we can have fun with others while we eat.

A TIME TO SHARE
1. *What are these boys and girls doing?*
2. *How do you know they are having fun?*
3. *What are some fun things you like to do on a picnic?*
4. *Why are you thankful that God helps us have fun when we eat?*

WHAT DO YOU SEE?
How many kinds of food can you find? Where is this picnic? How do you know it is not in the woods?

125

Listen! What Do You Hear?

Growing God's Way: We learn to hear many wonderful sounds as we grow God's way.

Do you hear what I hear? There are some birds singing outside this boy's window. Listen! Puppy is giving some happy little barks. The boy hears these good things, even though he is listening to some music on his cassette player. Before long he will hear Mother's voice. She will call him to come to eat. He will hear Father read a Bible story tonight. Do you hear some of these things too? God gave us two ears to hear the wonderful sounds around us. Let's listen carefully.

A TIME TO SHARE
1. *What sounds does the boy hear? What are some sounds you hear each day?*
2. *Do you hear with your eyes or ears? What special things do you do with your eyes, your nose, and your mouth?*

WHAT DO YOU SEE?
Where is the music coming from? Point to the cassette player. Point to some things that tell you this is a boy's room.

Talking to Jesus

Growing God's Way: Jesus wants us to talk with Him often.

Do you see that tree? It looks like any other tree, doesn't it? But it helped a man see Jesus. Zaccheus heard that Jesus was coming to town. He wanted to see Him. But Zaccheus was short. He could not see over the others in the crowd. So Zaccheus climbed this tree. Then he saw Jesus. He even talked with Jesus. Don't you think Zaccheus was glad for this tree?

A TIME TO SHARE
1. *Why did Zaccheus climb this tree?*
2. *Who did he see when he was there?*
3. *Do you like to talk with Jesus each day? What do you tell Him?*

WHAT DO YOU SEE?
Point to the tree. Point to the town where Zaccheus lived. Which house do you think Zaccheus lived in?

WHAT DO YOU SEE?
What do you see that tells you this is not the city? How will Father and the boy get home? Will they fly or drive a car? What will they do?

Are You Brave?
Are You Afraid?

Growing God's Way: God teaches us to be afraid of things that may hurt us, and to be brave when we should.

Look at that big bull over there. Do you see it? Father and the boy see it. Do you think they are afraid? Yes, they are. They are afraid to walk into the pasture with the bull. God teaches us to be afraid of things like a big bull. He would not want us to walk foolishly into a pasture with this animal. There are times when we should be brave. But we should never be careless or foolish, should we?

A TIME TO SHARE
1. *What do you see in the pasture?*
2. *Would you be afraid of the bull? Why?*
3. *Would you be afraid of a chicken or a duck? Why not? God protects you by making you afraid of things that could hurt you.*

WHAT DO YOU SEE?
Who do you think made this popcorn? Did Mother? Did Father? Why not? Who will pay for the popcorn? Mother has a purse with money in it. She could have paid for it. But you can see that she didn't. Now who will eat the popcorn?

It Smells Good, and Tastes Good

Growing God's Way: God helps us smell and taste good things.

Do you like to smell hot buttered popcorn? You can smell it before you taste it. This family smelled the popcorn before they saw the cart. It smelled so good. That's why they are buying some. Now they will eat it. Do you think it will taste good? God gives us a nose to smell good things. He gives us a mouth to taste good things. Are you thankful for these things?

A TIME TO SHARE
1. *What are these people buying?*
2. *Point to your nose. Do you smell with it or taste with it? Point to your mouth. What do you do with that?*

I Love My Puppy

Growing God's Way: God helps us love special people and special things.

Do you like to play with your puppy or kitty? This boy is having fun with his puppy. You can see that. The puppy is having fun with the boy too. Do you think the boy loves the puppy? Do you think the puppy loves the boy? Who else does the boy love? Do you think the boy loves Mother in a different way than Puppy? Can you name some people or things you love?

WHAT DO YOU SEE?
How many smiles do you see? Why is Mother smiling? Why is the boy smiling? Puppy isn't smiling but he is happy. How do you know?

A TIME TO SHARE
1. Who takes care of Puppy?
2. Who takes care of the boy?
3. Who takes care of Mother?
4. How does God take good care of us?

Some Food Grows on Trees

Growing God's Way: God gives us good food, and some of it grows on trees.

It's time for breakfast. This girl is going to have her favorite breakfast this morning. Mother will give her orange juice, scrambled eggs, toast, and bacon. Doesn't that sound good? The girl thinks so. Mother tells her that one of these things comes from trees. Do you know which one? Do eggs come from trees? Where do we get them? Does bacon come from trees? Where do we get that? What about the bread for the toast? Where do we get the wheat flour for that? Could it be the oranges?

A TIME TO SHARE
1. Which meal is Mother making?
2. What will they have?
3. Are oranges a fruit, grain, or nut? What kind of trees do they grow on?
4. You may like to thank God for oranges right now. Will you?

WHAT DO YOU SEE?
How many glasses do you see? Do you think someone else will eat breakfast with Mother and the girl? Who could that be? How many oranges do you see? What kinds of kitchen tools do you see? What did Mother use to get the orange juice?

Saying I Love You

Growing God's Way: ***It's important to tell our family members that we love them, even if they are far away.***

Did you hear the phone ringing? This girl did. When she answered it she heard the voice of someone she loves. Who do you think that is? Do you like to talk on the phone to Grandfather or Grandmother? What about an uncle or aunt, or a cousin? This girl and boy can't see their grandparents very often. They live far away. But they like to talk with them by phone. And they are always sure to tell each other, "I love you." That's a good idea, isn't it?

WHAT DO YOU SEE?
Whose picture do you see? Is the girl smiling or frowning? This tells you that she loves the person who is calling. Why do you think it is Grandfather or Grandmother?

A TIME TO SHARE
1. *Name some family members that you love.*
2. *Which family members do you talk with by phone?*
3. *Do you ever tell your family members, "I love you"?*

Giving My Best to God

Growing God's Way: God has given much to us, so we should give our best to Him.

This lady is smiling, so you know she is happy about something. Do you think she is happy she can give that money? She is giving it to help God's people do His work, so she knows God will be pleased. That makes her happy. Do you like to give money at church? When you do, you know that God is pleased. And that should make you happy.

A TIME TO SHARE
1. *What is this woman doing?*
2. *Why is she happy doing this?*
3. *Why should we give money to God?*

WHAT DO YOU SEE?
Where is this woman putting her money? That strange-looking box is like a collection plate in your church. People took money from it to use in God's house.

Something to Eat This Morning

Growing God's Way: God helps us get three good meals each day.

Ummmmm. You can almost smell that toast, can't you? Mother is putting butter on the hot toast. Next she will put on some jam. Then the boy will eat breakfast with Mother. Today he will also eat lunch and dinner. The boy is glad that God helps him get three good meals each day. That is part of God's wonderful plan to take care of us.

A TIME TO SHARE
1. What meal is the boy about to eat? How do you know?
2. What other kind of food do people usually eat for breakfast? What do you sometimes eat for lunch? What do you sometimes eat for dinner?

WHAT DO YOU SEE?
Where is the toaster? What does the toaster do? Point to the butter. Where is the jam? Can you find two pieces of toast?

Autumn Is a Special Time

Growing God's Way: God gives us four seasons each year, and autumn is one of those special times.

Do you see the beautiful colors in the leaves? The boy and girl see them. They are glad for the beautiful colors. Now they know that autumn is here. God gives us four special seasons each year. He gives us spring, summer, autumn, and winter. In many parts of the world, God changes the way things grow in these special seasons. Most of us do not plant our gardens in autumn or winter. We do that in the spring. Are you glad for autumn? Or do you call it fall?

A TIME TO SHARE
1. *What are the boy and girl doing?*
2. *What special things do you do in the autumn? What special food do you eat?*
3. *Do you have a favorite holiday in the autumn? What is it?*

WHAT DO YOU SEE?
How do you know this is not spring? How do you know it is not winter? Point to some yellow leaves. Point to some red leaves. Can you find the squirrel?

135

Making Good Things with Mother

Growing God's Way: God has planned for us to do good things with our parents.

Look what Mother and her girl are going to do! Today is the day for pancakes. Mother could make them by herself. But her girl thinks it would be fun to help her. She even has an apron like Mother. Don't you think it is fun to make good things with Mother or Father?

WHAT DO YOU SEE?
Mother and the girl have nine things which will help them make pancakes. Point to each one and tell what it is.

A TIME TO SHARE
1. *Why do you think Mother and the girl are both smiling? Why don't they look sad?*
2. *What good things do you like to do with Mother or Father?*

We're Glad for Pumpkins

Growing God's Way: God gives us four special seasons of the year.

God made four special seasons of the year. Can you name all of them? In most parts of the country we plant seeds in the spring. The warm summer sun smiles on them and they grow to be green plants. This pumpkin came from pumpkin seeds that this boy and girl planted last spring. During the summer big pumpkin vines grew with little green pumpkins on them. Now look! This big orange pumpkin tells us that autumn, or fall, has come. Pumpkins don't grow in the winter, do they? Do you know why?

A TIME TO SHARE
1. *Why don't plants grow in the winter in most parts of the country?*
2. *What season was it when the boy and girl planted the pumpkin seeds? What happened during the summer?*
3. *How do you know it is autumn, or fall, now? Who planned for the seasons?*

WHAT DO YOU SEE?
What month do you think this is? Why do you think so? Is the pumpkin face happy or sad? How many faces do you see? Point to four faces.

Where Do We Get Our Bread?

***Growing God's Way:** We get bread from special plants and animals. God helped these plants and animals grow.*

Do you smell that bread baking in the oven? What is so wonderful as fresh bread that Mother makes? You can see how much fun this boy and girl are having as they eat the bread. The butter melts into the bread and the strawberry jam adds a special taste. But where did Mother's bread come from? Mother mixed flour, milk, sugar, and butter together to make her bread dough, with some other things too. The flour came from grains of wheat that grew on wheat plants. Cows ate grass and gave the milk. Most sugar comes from plants that look like cornstalks.

A TIME TO SHARE
1. What is Mother doing now?
2. What are the boy and girl doing?
3. What three plants give us bread? What animal helps us have bread?
4. Who helped the plants and animals grow and give us what we need? Have you thanked God for doing this?

WHAT DO YOU SEE?
Point to each thing Mother used to make the bread. Can you name each one? Can you tell how each was used to make the bread?

Time for Lunch!

Growing God's Way: God helps us get food to eat wherever we live.

Have you ever seen a lunch like this before? You probably would not want to carry this basket of bread and fish to school, would you? What would your friends say if you did? But this boy was glad for the bread and fish. All his friends ate bread and fish for lunch. His neighbors raised wheat for the bread, and caught fish in the big lake nearby. They had no grocery stores, so they ate what they grew in their fields and gardens. Or they ate food from animals that grew nearby. Wherever we live, there are special foods that God gives. We should thank Him for the good food He sends to us. This boy will give his lunch to Jesus. Jesus will feed many people with it. Jesus is God's Son, so He can do something special like that.

WHAT DO YOU SEE?
How many rolls of bread do you see? How many fish do you see? This boy will share his lunch with Jesus. Jesus will feed many people with it. Can you find these people?

A TIME TO SHARE
1. *How is this lunch different from your lunch?*
2. *Jesus fed many people with the boy's lunch. How can Jesus do this? Who is He?*

Something We Can Do Together

Growing God's Way: Families can do many fun things together. That's how they grow to love each other more.

Now here is something fun to do on a fall day! Have you ever been on a hayride? This family likes to go on a hayride together. They laugh and talk. They may even toss some hay here and there. This family thinks a hayride together is family fun together. When they go home they will have hot chocolate and cookies. Then they will talk about the fun time they had on their hayride. Jesus wants to see families have fun together. He knows that helps them love each other more.

WHAT DO YOU SEE?
Why do you think this is in the country? Why is it not in the city? Point to the four wheels. Which member of the family is driving?

A TIME TO SHARE
1. What are some things you see on a hayride? What do you smell? What do you hear?
2. Why is it fun to go on a hayride as a family? Why is Jesus pleased to see families do things like this together?

We Are Thankful for Good Gifts

Growing God's Way: We should be thankful for the good things God gives us in the fall.

It's that time of year again. What fun to buy pumpkins and corn for special fall days. Someone planted seeds this spring. They pulled out the weeds this summer. But God sent the rain and sunshine. He made the pumpkins and corn grow. God made other wonderful things grow too. Now it is time to harvest them. Are you thankful for God's good gifts in the fall? Would you like to thank Him now?

A TIME TO SHARE
1. *What is this family buying?*
2. *What do you think they will do with their pumpkins and corn? What would you do with them if you bought some?*
3. *What would you like to say to God about these good gifts?*

WHAT DO YOU SEE?
What season of the year is this? Point to some things that tell you it is fall. How many pumpkins can you find? Which pumpkin did the girl choose? Which one did the boy choose? Which one did Father choose?

Having Fun While We Work

Growing God's Way: *We please God by having fun together while we work. We could be grumbling and complaining, and God would not like that.*

This family is working. You can see that. But do you see anyone grumbling or complaining? That would not be fun at all. Everyone is having fun. Did you know that it can be fun to work? Did you know that God is pleased when we turn our work into fun?

A TIME TO SHARE
1. *What kind of work are they doing?*
2. *Why do you think this is fun for them?*
3. *What were some chores you did this week? How did you make them fun to do?*

WHAT DO YOU SEE?
Where did these leaves come from? Can you find the tree? How do you know this is not winter? What season is this? How do you know?

Special Food for Special Days

Growing God's Way: God gives us special food for special days. We should remember to thank Him.

There is something special about this day. Do you know what it is? This family is getting ready for Thanksgiving dinner. Mother has cooked a turkey and other good things to eat. The boy and girl have helped too. They put the dishes on the table, and helped Mother get things ready for dinner. Now Father is going to do something too. What do you think he will do? Do you think the family will remember to thank God for this special day?

A TIME TO SHARE
1. *What special time is this? What special food is this?*
2. *What other special days have special foods? Can you think of some?*
3. *God gives us special food to eat. Be sure to thank Him.*

WHAT DO YOU SEE?
Point to some things that tell you this is a special day. Can you name each of these things?

A Hug and a Kiss

Growing God's Way: There are times to give a hug and a kiss and to say, "I love you."

Father is home! You can see that he has been away for a few days. Guess who gets the first hug and kiss? And who is there for the second one? Do you suppose Father and Mother are saying, "I love you"? Do you think Father and his girl will say that too?

WHAT DO YOU SEE?
What is that next to Father? Does he take this suitcase to work? Where does he take it? How do you know that Father has been on a trip? Why do you think he is coming home now?

A TIME TO SHARE
1. Are you glad for a special hug from someone you love? Why?
2. What does a hug or a kiss tell you?
3. Why should we say "I love you" to our family? Why do you think that Jesus is pleased when we do?

Being Kind to One Another

Growing God's Way: God wants us to be kind to one another. That's the right way to grow to please Him.

Look at that tower the boy and girl are making. You can see that they have worked to make it. But something bad could happen here. That boy with the ball could cause trouble. What would you like to say to him right now? What would you say to him if he throws the ball?

A TIME TO SHARE
1. *What are the boy and girl making?*
2. *How do you know the boy and girl are thinking about Jesus? What word do you see on the blocks?*

WHAT DO YOU SEE?
How many blocks can you count? What letters do you see on the blocks?

The Lost Sheep

Growing God's Way: Jesus is the Good Shepherd. When we wander away from Him, He will help us find the way back.

This foolish sheep is alone. He should be with the shepherd and his other sheep. But this sheep wandered away and doesn't know how to get back. The shepherd knows the way. He will find this lost sheep. Then he will lead it back to be with him. Aren't you glad the shepherd will do this? Jesus said you and I are His sheep. He loves us. He says He is our Good Shepherd. He wants to take care of us.

WHAT DO YOU SEE?
How many sheep do you see? Where are the others? Where is the shepherd?

A TIME TO SHARE
1. *Why isn't this sheep home with the shepherd and the other sheep?*
2. *Who will come to find this sheep?*
3. *How is this sheep like us? How is the shepherd like Jesus?*

Time for School!

***Growing God's Way:** Aren't you glad when Mother does special things for you, such as helping you get ready for school?*

Look at that clock! This boy has only fifteen minutes to get to school. He must hurry! Mother knows he is late. You can see that she is there with his lunch and books. Mother is glad to do something special for her boy. Some mothers have to work, so they can't be there when their boy or girl leaves for school or comes home. They love their boy or girl just as much as this mother. So they do other special things for their boy or girl. What special things does your mother do for you?

WHAT DO YOU SEE?
What time is it? Why do you think this is morning and not night? What is Mother holding in her hands? What will the boy do with them?

A TIME TO SHARE
1. *What is the boy doing?*
2. *Why do you think he is glad for Mother's help?*
3. *What special things does Mother or Father do for you? What special things do you do for them?*

147

Listen to the Noise!

Growing God's Way: We need to think of others when we want to make noise. God wants us to be kind to others and not do things that make them unhappy.

It's fun to blow a horn, isn't it? But it's more fun to blow a horn in the right place. This boy is having fun with his horn. But Father is not having fun. Brother is not having fun either. Now look at Puppy. Do you think he is having fun? This boy should go outside to blow on his horn. Don't you think that would be the kind thing to do? Would you like to tell him to do that?

WHAT DO YOU SEE?
How many faces do you see? How many happy faces do you see? Is this inside the house or outside the house? How do you know?

A TIME TO SHARE
1. Why are none of the faces here happy?
2. What would make them happier?
3. *What do you think Jesus would say to this boy? What would you say to him?*

Something Good Together

Growing God's Way: Doing good things together is a special part of growing up.

This girl has just come home from school. You know how that feels, don't you? Mother knows. She was once a little girl too. That's why Mother has some cookies and milk ready for her girl. Of course, Mother will eat some cookies and milk with her girl. They will talk about the things that happened at school. The girl will want to know what happened at home too. Doing fun things together is a wonderful part of growing God's way. Aren't you glad when you can do special things with Mother or Father?

A TIME TO SHARE
1. *What do you like to do when you come home from school?*
2. *Are you glad when you can do something special with Mother or Father? Do you think Jesus is pleased when you do?*

WHAT DO YOU SEE?
What room is this? How do you know it is not the living room? What did the girl forget to do when she came home? Would you like to tell her to hang something up instead of throwing it on the floor?

New Shoes

***Growing God's Way:** Growing into new shoes and clothes reminds us of the way our bodies are growing. We must be sure our love for God is growing just as fast.*

New shoe time is a fun time, isn't it? This boy and girl are having fun getting new shoes. Mother is glad to buy new shoes for her boy and girl. She knows their feet are growing so they must have bigger shoes. New shoe time is a time when we see how much our feet have grown. New clothes time is a time when we see how much our bodies have grown. These are also good times to ask ourselves how much our love for God has grown this year. Would you like to ask that now?

A TIME TO SHARE

1. What are the girl and boy doing?
2. What will they learn about growing feet? Are their feet larger or smaller than last year? Why?
3. Has your love for God grown this year? How do you know?

WHAT DO YOU SEE?
What kind of store is this? How do you know? How do you know this is not a grocery store? Point to some boxes with shoes in them. Point to some things that help us take care of shoes. What are they?

Obey Jesus!

Growing God's Way: Jesus knows what is best for us, so we should obey Him.

Do you see all those fish in the net? Someone caught them. Some of Jesus' friends went fishing. They fished all night. But they could not catch any fish. Then Jesus told them where to put their nets. When they listened to Jesus, they caught all those fish. Jesus knows what is best for us, doesn't He? That's why we should obey Him.

A TIME TO SHARE
1. Who caught those fish?
2. Who knew where to find the fish?
3. How did Jesus know this?
4. Why should we obey Jesus?

WHAT DO YOU SEE?
Do you see the floats around the edge of the net? They kept one edge of the net on top of the water. The other edge sank into the water to catch the fish. Can you count the fish? How many are there?

WHAT DO YOU SEE?
Where is this? Is it on a farm? Is it in a living room? How do you know? Do you see one airplane flying? Do you see one that is not flying?

Someone Is Coming Home
Growing God's Way: We are glad when we can be together with those we love.

Look! Do you see that airplane coming in? Father is on it. You can see how excited Mother and the boy are to welcome him home. It's not much fun when someone we love has gone away on a trip, is it? But it is fun when that person comes home. When we love someone, we want to be with that person. When we love Jesus, we want to take time to talk with Him and read what He says in the Bible. Do you do that?

A TIME TO SHARE
1. *Why are Mother and the boy waving at this airplane? Who is on it?*
2. *Will Father be happy to be home? Why?*
3. *Do you like to be with people you love? Why?*

Grandfather's Best Story

***Growing God's Way:** Grandfathers and grandmothers can help us grow the way God wants. Is that why we like to listen to them?*

Do you like to visit Grandfather and Grandmother? Does your grandfather ever tell you stories? This boy likes to come to Grandfather's house. He likes to listen to Grandfather's stories. This may be the best story ever. You can see that it is a cold winter night. What could be better than sitting by the fire with Grandfather, listening to a special story? What do you think Grandmother is doing now? Could she be in the kitchen, making hot chocolate or popcorn?

A TIME TO SHARE
1. *Why does the boy look so happy?*
2. *What kind of story do you think Grandfather is telling?*
3. *Why are grandfathers and grandmothers special? What do you like best about your grandfather or grandmother?*

WHAT DO YOU SEE?
How do you know this is winter? What do you see that you would not see in the summer? How many coats and boots do you see? Who wore those coats here?

WHAT DO YOU SEE?
How many balls of yarn do you see? What else do you see that will help Mother knit with the yarn? Who else is having fun with the yarn?

Making Something Special
Growing God's Way: We learn from Mother and Father how to make special things.

Mother is making something special. What do you think it is? Could it be a cap for the girl to wear? Perhaps it is a scarf. The girl likes to watch Mother make special things. Mother will teach her how to knit too. Then the girl will be able to do it. Mother and Father teach us how to make many special things. God is pleased when we learn to make special things. He made some special things for us too, didn't He?

A TIME TO SHARE
1. *What do you think Mother is making?*
2. *Who will learn to knit too?*
3. *What have Mother and Father taught you to make? Did you thank them for doing this?*

I'm Scared!

***Growing God's Way:** When we are afraid, it helps to talk with Jesus.*

Have you ever heard strange noises in the night? This boy did. He was afraid. He even said, "I'm scared!" Mother and Father were sleeping, so they did not hear him. So the boy prayed to Jesus. He asked Jesus to help him. Now look! The boy has found his flashlight. He will not be afraid anymore. Do you know why?

WHAT DO YOU SEE?
What was the noise that made the boy afraid? Do you think he will be afraid now? Why not? How do you know this is night?

A TIME TO SHARE
1. *What are some things that have made you afraid? What did you do?*
2. *Why should you pray to Jesus when you are afraid? Will you do that next time?*

My Friends Help Me

Growing God's Way: *My friends and I like to help each other.*

Here is something you don't see every day. The man in the basket is Paul. He is in trouble in this city. Some men want to kill him. But Paul has some friends. Do you see what they are doing? Paul cannot go through the gate to leave this city. Some men are waiting at the gate to kill him. His friends are keeping him safe by letting him down the wall of the city. He does not need to go through the gate. As soon as Paul gets to the ground, he will go to another city. Paul was glad for friends who helped. Are you glad for friends who help you? Are you glad you can help your friends? Jesus is glad when friends help each other.

A TIME TO SHARE
1. *What are Paul's friends doing for him?*
2. *Who are some of your friends?*
3. *What do your friends do to help you? What do you do to help your friends?*
4. *What does Jesus do for you? What do you do to help Jesus?*

WHAT DO YOU SEE?
How are Paul's friends helping him escape from the city? Do you see the wall of the city? Do you see the window? Which man is Paul?

Talking Together

Growing God's Way: I grow God's way when I can talk about Him with Mother or Father.

This girl and her mother are having a special talk together. They like to talk about many things. They talk about school. They talk about the things Mother did today. And they talk about things they will do together. But they also talk about God and the wonderful things He has done for them. The girl is so glad that she can talk with Mother about God. She knows Mother will tell her how to do right things. That's always good to know, isn't it?

A TIME TO SHARE
1. *Who are these two people?*
2. *What do you think they are talking about?*
3. *Do you like to talk with Mother? Why?*

WHAT DO YOU SEE?
Do you see a light in this room? What is it? Jesus tells us that we should shine like lights. How can we shine for Jesus? When you are kind to your brother, are you shining for Jesus? Tell of another way you can shine for Jesus.

Snowtime Is Grow Time

Growing God's Way: We grow God's way when we enjoy the wonderful world He made for us.

Look! It's snowing! That's the time to put on hats and coats and boots and go outdoors to play. What do you like to do in the snow? This boy and girl like to chase the snowflakes. They will build a snowman. Then they will go sledding on the hill. Snow time is the time to play outside. Snow time is the time to get lots of fresh air and exercise. Do you think this boy and girl will eat a good dinner tonight? They will grow stronger because they played outside today. God planned for us to get fresh air and exercise. That's the way He helps us grow strong.

A TIME TO SHARE
1. *Who makes the snowflakes?*
2. *Why is playing in the snow a time to help us grow? What does it do for us?*
3. *What do you like to do in the snow?*
4. *Do you thank God for snowtime?*

WHAT DO YOU SEE?
How do you know this is winter? What would you not see in the summer? How do you know the boy and girl are outdoors? Who is indoors?

It's Fun to Do Things Together

Growing God's Way: We grow God's way as we learn to do things with others.

It's fun to play outdoors. But some days are too hot. Some days are too cold. Some days are too rainy. And sometimes we like to do fun things with friends and family, even when the weather is good. This boy and girl are having fun with their crayons. They think it is fun to color in their coloring books together. We grow God's way as we learn to do things with others. That's because we learn to share, and please others. God wants us to learn to do those things, doesn't He?

A TIME TO SHARE
1. *Do you think the boy and girl are having fun? How do you know?*
2. *What are they doing? Do you like to color in coloring books? Do you like to do this with someone? Why?*

WHAT DO YOU SEE?
Is it summer or winter? How do you know? Is it morning or afternoon? How do you know?

Let Me Help You

Growing God's Way: We grow God's way when we learn to help others. That's how we please Jesus.

Do you like to shovel snow from your sidewalk? Someone has to do it. Father started to do it. But look who is helping! Father is glad that his boy wants to help. He does not shovel as much snow as Father. But he is helping. Don't you think Jesus is pleased when we are helpers? He knows we will learn to grow His way. That's something good to learn, isn't it?

WHAT DO YOU SEE?
What is that big thing coming down the street? Why can't it shovel the sidewalk for Father? Why can't the boy use that thing to push the snow from the streets?

A TIME TO SHARE
1. *What is the boy doing? Who is he helping?*
2. *Why do you think the boy is happy?*
3. *What do you like to help Father or Mother do? Why is it fun to help them?*
4. *Would you like to please Jesus? What are some things you can do?*

Jesus Is with Me

Growing God's Way: Wherever we go we must remember that Jesus is with us, and we should remember to tell others about Him.

This looks like fun, doesn't it? How would you like to be sailing on this ship? It wasn't much fun for Paul. He was a prisoner on this ship. He couldn't go to any other place, or do anything different. He had to stay on this ship and do what soldiers told him. But Paul knew that Jesus was with him. He remembered to tell the people on the ship about Jesus. That's good for us to remember too. We may be doing things we don't like. Or we may be in a place we don't like. But Jesus is still with us. And He wants us to tell others there about Him.

A TIME TO SHARE
1. Who is on this ship? Who is with Paul on this ship?
2. Is Paul having fun sailing?
3. What will Paul remember to do here?

WHAT DO YOU SEE?
How many men do you see on the ship? How many of them do you think Paul told about Jesus? Which way is the ship going?

Learning to Tell Time

Growing God's Way: God wants us to learn to tell time so that we can use the time He gives us wisely.

Do you know how to tell time? This girl is learning that now. Father is teaching her. The big hand is on 12, and the little hand is on 5. What time is it? Good! You are right. It is 5 o'clock. This clock has a little bird called a cuckoo. It will say "cuckoo" five times now. How many times will it say "cuckoo" when it is 8 o'clock? God gives us each the same amount of time every day. It's important to learn to tell time on watches and clocks. That will help us use wisely the time God gives us. And that will help us grow God's way.

WHAT DO YOU SEE?
What number is the big hand pointing to? What number is the little hand pointing to? How many times will the bird say "cuckoo" now?

A TIME TO SHARE
1. *What is Father helping the girl learn?*
2. *Why should we learn to tell time?*
3. *Have you thanked God for giving you 24 hours to live today? Would you do that now? Will you try to use those hours wisely?*

God Paints Beautiful Pictures

Growing God's Way: God paints many beautiful pictures for us to see. We should enjoy them and thank Him for them.

This is a bright, cold winter day. You can see that, can't you? But look what God did last night. He painted some beautiful pictures for these boys and girls to enjoy. Do you see the frost pictures God painted on the window? This boy and girl are looking at all the beautiful designs in the frost. Do you like to do that? Now look at the beautiful pictures God painted with the snow. Everywhere you look, you see something beautiful that God did with the snow. He is a wonderful artist, isn't He?

WHAT DO YOU SEE?
What do you see that you would not see in the summer? Why wouldn't you see these things in the summer?

A TIME TO SHARE
1. *Have you ever seen frost on a window? Where was that? What did the frost look like?*
2. *Who made the frost? What other wonderful things did God make?*

163

Someone to Help Me

***Growing God's Way:** God gave me a mother to help me. She helps me grow God's way.*

Guess what day this is. At this boy's house it's Monday. That's when Mother washes and irons the laundry. What would this boy do without Mother to help keep him clean? Who would wash his clothes and iron them? Who would buy him new clothes? Who would help him zip up zippers that get stuck? Who would help him do a hundred other things? This boy thanked God for Mother this morning. Did you?

A TIME TO SHARE
1. What is this mother doing?
2. Make a list of all the things your mother does for you. Will you thank her now for doing these things?
3. Will you thank God now for your mother?

WHAT DO YOU SEE?
What kinds of clothing do you see? Point to each one and tell what it is. What are some things that will help Mother wash the clothes? Point to each one and tell what it does. How many zippers do you see?

Look Who Came to Our House!

Growing God's Way: God made many beautiful birds. We learn more about them when we watch them.

What do you see outside the window? These birds are glad for the seed. They get hungry, just as you do. But it is hard for them to find food in the winter. That's why they like to come to this bird feeder. The boy and his mother are glad too. They like to watch the birds. God has made many beautiful birds. Isn't it wonderful when you can watch some birds just outside your window? This is a good time to thank God for making beautiful birds, isn't it?

A TIME TO SHARE

1. *What are these birds doing?*
2. *Why did they come to this place?*
3. *Can you make a beautiful bird? Why not? Who makes the birds? Have you thanked God for beautiful birds? Would you like to do that now?*

WHAT DO YOU SEE?
How many birds do you see here? Point to each one. What kind is the red bird? What kind is the blue bird? How do you know this is winter?

Someone Who Loves Me

Growing God's Way: God gives us grandmothers and grandfathers to love us and help take care of us.

Do you like to go to Grandmother's and Grandfather's house? This boy does. You can see that he is having fun already. He doesn't even have his coat and hat off yet. But he has found a special place to play. Of course he had lots of hugs and kisses when he came in. Grandparents are special people, aren't they? Grandsons and granddaughters are special people too! That's why God planned for grandparents and grandchildren. Don't you think God had a wonderful plan?

WHAT DO YOU SEE?
How many people can you find in this picture? Who is each one? How do you know? What toys do you see? What time of the year is this? How do you know?

A TIME TO SHARE
1. *Why is the boy so happy?*
2. *Why are Grandfather and Grandmother happy?*
3. *What good things do grandparents do for us? Why should you thank God for your grandparents?*

A Warm Place to Sleep

Growing God's Way: God gives us a warm place to sleep. Are you thankful for your nice warm bed?

How would you like to sleep in this bed every night? Baby Jesus slept in it. This bed was called a manger. That's where cows ate. There was no other place for Baby Jesus to sleep. Mary and Joseph could not find a better place. But you don't have to sleep in a manger tonight, do you? Do you thank God for your nice warm bed?

A TIME TO SHARE
1. *Who slept in this bed?*
2. *What was it called?*
3. *Why did He sleep here?*
4. *Would you like to thank God for your nice bed now?*

WHAT DO YOU SEE?
Do you see the long cloth? Mary wrapped the cloth around Baby Jesus. Then she put Him here to sleep. Do you see the straw? Where is the manger?

167

Going Places Together

***Growing God's Way:** We go places together as a family. As we do, we talk about God together.*

Do you like to go shopping with Mother or Father? It's fun to go special places together, isn't it? This family likes to go to the store together. Sometimes they laugh and talk about funny things. But they often talk together about God too. Riding this escalator reminded them of Jacob's ladder. Do you know why? At the grocery store they talked about God giving them good food. And at the clothing store they talked about God giving them good clothes to wear. Now you know why this family has fun as they go to special places together.

WHAT DO YOU SEE?
Is this family riding up or down? How do you know? What does this store sell on the floor they are leaving? Have they bought anything yet? How do you know?

A TIME TO SHARE
1. *What is this family doing together?*
2. *What do they talk about together?*
3. *What would you say if you were here?*

Grandmother's Special Gift

Growing God's Way: *In our family we like to give special gifts to each other. The most special gifts are those we make, or something good we do for others.*

Do you see what Grandmother has made for this girl? Grandmother is so happy that she could make such a beautiful gift for her. You can see that she loves the girl very much. You can see also that the girl is happy that Grandmother has made this beautiful quilt for her. She will keep that quilt for many years. Whenever the quilt keeps her warm, she will think of Grandmother. God is pleased when we give special gifts to one another or do special things for one another. Do you know why?

WHAT DO YOU SEE?
What kind of machine do you see? How did Grandmother use this machine to make her quilt? Can you find the thread? How did that help to make the quilt? What else do you see that helped make the quilt?

A TIME TO SHARE
1. *Who is happy? Why is each person happy?*
2. *What special gifts do you and your family give each other? What special things do you do for each other?*
3. *Why is God pleased when we give good gifts or do special things for each other?*

The Right Food for the Right Day

Growing God's Way: God helps us get just the right kind of food for the right time.

This is not a hot summer day, is it? You can see that it is a cold winter day. But isn't it fun on a cold winter morning to drink hot chocolate? Isn't it fun to eat hot pancakes or waffles, or eggs and bacon? You wouldn't want to have ice cubes or frozen corn on a morning like this, would you? Isn't it wonderful how God helps us have special foods for cold winter days and other special foods for hot summer days? He's a wonderful God, isn't He?

WHAT DO YOU SEE?
How do you know this is hot chocolate? Point to the cups with the hot chocolate in them. How many are there? Can you find the marshmallows? Can you find the milk? How do these help make hot chocolate just right?

A TIME TO SHARE
1. *What kind of day is this? Why does hot chocolate taste good today? Why would it not taste as good on a hot summer day?*
2. *What are some fun things this family may do today? What do you like to do on a cold winter day?*

What Should We Make Today?

Growing God's Way: God is pleased when mothers and daughters make things together.

You can see that this mother and daughter are having fun together. Today is the day to make cookies. Sometimes it's more fun to make them than to eat them. But that's because it's so much fun to make things together. Last week Mother and the girl made a rag doll together. Next week they will do something else that is special. They like to talk about many things when they work or play together. Do you suppose they talk about Jesus? Do you suppose they talk about the Bible, God's Word?

A TIME TO SHARE
1. *What are Mother and the girl doing? What is Mother holding?*
2. *What do you think Mother and the girl are talking about? What would you like to talk about if you were here?*

WHAT DO YOU SEE?
Point to the different things that helped them make cookies. Can you tell what they are doing with each one?

A Gift for You

***Growing God's Way:** We grow God's way when we give good gifts to each other. God gives us special gifts, and He wants us to give special gifts too.*

What would it be like if you never gave gifts and no one ever gave you gifts? That wouldn't be much fun, would it? But here is a special friend with a special gift for a special day. Isn't it fun to open the door and see a smiling friend with a gift? The girl who lives here is happy that her friend loves her enough to bring her a gift. Do you think that she has a gift for her friend too?

A TIME TO SHARE
1. *What special time of the year is this? How do you know?*
2. *Why do you think this girl is giving a gift to her friend?*
3. *Why do you like to give good gifts? What good gifts has God given you? What good gifts have you given Him?*

WHAT DO YOU SEE?
Point to some things that tell you this is winter. How many smiling faces do you see? Why are they smiling?

Going God's Way

Growing God's Way: Growing God's way is going where God wants us to go and doing what God wants us to do.

That must be the brightest star that ever shone in the sky. It was a special star. God put it there to guide the wise men to Jesus. They knew that God sent this star. That's why they followed it. When they did, the star led them to Jesus. We grow God's way when we do what God wants us to do, and go where God wants us to go. Do you think the wise men would tell us that?

A TIME TO SHARE
1. *Where are these men going? What are they following?*
2. *Where will this star lead them?*
3. *Why should we go where God wants us to go? Why should we do what God wants us to do?*

WHAT DO YOU SEE?
How many men do you see? What are they riding? Point to the star. Who made this special star? Why did He make it?

Something Warm to Wear

Growing God's Way: God gives us new clothes to keep us warm.

Brrr. It's cold outside. When the wind blows, the cold air nips at your nose. That's why this girl is glad for her new mittens. They keep her hands warm. When she puts her warm mittens up to her face, they help keep her face warm too. But next summer she will not wear her mittens, will she? Do you know why?

WHAT DO YOU SEE?
How do you know that this is a cold winter day? Point to some things that tell you this. How would these things be different on a hot summer day?

A TIME TO SHARE
1. *How would you feel if you had no warm clothes? What would happen?*
2. *Are you thankful for warm clothes on a cold winter day? Have you thanked your parents for them? Will you do that now? Have you thanked God for them? Will you do that now?*

Do You Hear What I Hear?

Growing God's Way: **God gives many wonderful sounds for us to hear. We should be thankful for each one.**

Listen to the crackling sound of the fire in the fireplace. Do you hear it? Listen to the tick-tock of the clock. Do you hear it? Listen to the clock each hour. It goes bong, bong, bong. Do you hear it? Listen to the soft tick-tick, tick-tick of Grandfather's watch. Do you hear it? Listen to Grandfather laugh and talk. This girl loves to hear his voice. It reminds her that Grandfather loves her very much. Sometimes Grandfather says, "I love you." Aren't you glad that you can hear wonderful sounds like these?

A TIME TO SHARE
1. *How many sounds does this girl hear? Can you name each one?*
2. *How many sounds do you hear each day? Can you name some of them?*
3. *Do you ever thank God that you can hear? Would you like to do that now?*

WHAT DO YOU SEE?
Point to each thing that makes a sound. What kind of sound does it make?

What Music Do You Play?

Growing God's Way: Do you sing or play a musical instrument? That's a wonderful way to grow God's way.

Listen to the bells. Do you see who is ringing them? These girls and boys are making music with the bells. If you have ever heard a handbell choir, you know about the beautiful music of the bells. Perhaps you play the piano, violin, or trumpet. You may sing well too. God helps us learn to play or sing. Sometimes we sing about Jesus. Or we may play a song that tells us about God's Word. Music is one of God's great gifts. It helps us grow God's way.

WHAT DO YOU SEE?
How many bells do you see? How many boys and girls are ringing the bells? What kind of building do you think this is? Why?

A TIME TO SHARE
1. *What are the girls and boys doing?*
2. *Why is Jesus pleased with their music?*
3. *What music do you play or sing? Why is Jesus pleased with your music?*

A Wonderful Time of the Year

Growing God's Way: Christmas is a wonderful time of the year because we learn about the Baby Jesus.

Do you see what this girl is doing? Now you know that it is a special time of the year. Is this Thanksgiving? Is it Easter? Is it Valentine's Day? What wonderful time of the year is this? How do you know? When the girl hangs her stocking, Mother will read a wonderful story from the Bible. The story is about the Baby Jesus. Christmas is a wonderful time of the year because we learn about Baby Jesus. We learn about the reason He came from heaven. Aren't you glad for Christmas? This girl and her mother are.

WHAT DO YOU SEE?
Point to each thing that tells you this is Christmas. What do you put in your house to show that it is Christmas?

A TIME TO SHARE
1. *What is the girl doing? Why is she doing this?*
2. *What may the girl find in her stocking? When will she find it?*
3. *Why do we give each other gifts at Christmas?*

Giving Gifts

Growing God's Way: We grow God's way when we learn to enjoy giving gifts as well as receiving them.

Do you like to get nice gifts for birthday or Christmas? Here are some special gifts that men gave to Baby Jesus. They did not wrap the gifts in wrapping paper. People did not do that when Jesus was a Baby. But the gifts are wonderful gifts anyway. One gift is gold. Another is a spice called frankincense. The third is a spice called myrrh. These gifts cost a lot of money. The men were glad to give Jesus the best gifts they could. Do you enjoy giving gifts? Do you like to give gifts to Jesus? When we learn that it is more fun to give gifts than to get them, we are growing God's way.

A TIME TO SHARE
1. *What kind of gifts do you see here?*
2. *Who gave these gifts? To whom did they give them?*
3. *Why is it more fun to give good gifts than to get them?*

WHAT DO YOU SEE?
What is in the box? How many pieces of gold can you find? What do you think is in the two jars? Who is the Baby?

Playing Outdoors

Growing God's Way: God planned for us to get plenty of fresh air and exercise.

Do you like to go sledding on a winter day? You can feel the wind on your face. You can feel the snow as it flies up from the runners. What is more exciting than sledding on a snowy hill? This boy's cheeks are rosy red from the cold and snow. But he will feel wonderful after this. It's good to get lots of fresh air and exercise, isn't it? What if you had to stay inside all your life? What if you could never play outside in the fresh air? Part of growing God's way is to get plenty of fresh air and exercise, isn't it?

A TIME TO SHARE
1. *How often do you play outside? Do you spend as much time playing outside as you do watching TV?*
2. *What are these boys and girls doing? Why is God pleased that they are doing this?*

WHAT DO YOU SEE?
How many boys and girls are playing here? How many are on saucers? How many are sliding on sleds? How many are pulling sleds up the hill? How do you know this is winter and not summer?

WHAT DO YOU SEE?
Where is the snowman? How many balls of snow did these friends have to make for the snowman? What is Father doing with the shovel?

Fun with My Friends
Growing God's Way: God planned for me to have fun with my friends.

What can you do with a few thousand snowflakes? Some boys and girls go sledding. Others throw snowballs at each other. And some make snowmen. Isn't it fun when you can do special things with your friends? These girls and boys like to play together. You can see that they are having fun. But that's the way God planned it. He wants friends to have fun together and do special things together. Don't you think God had a good idea?

A TIME TO SHARE
1. Are these girls and boys having fun? How do you know?
2. Why is it important to have friends? How do good friends help each other? Why do you think God planned for us to do good things with our friends?

Fun with My Family

Growing God's Way: God planned for me to have fun with my family.

Sometimes it's fun to play together with friends. And sometimes it's fun to play together with family. This is a time for fun with family. You can see how much fun this boy is having with Father. Sometimes this family goes on picnics. Sometimes they go hiking, or swimming, or making sandcastles on the beach. But now it is winter. So they have family fun in the snow. Aren't you glad God planned for families to have fun together?

A TIME TO SHARE
1. *What are Father and the boy doing?*
2. *Why do you think they are having fun?*
3. *Why did God plan for families to have fun together? What do you like to do with your family?*

WHAT DO YOU SEE?
Someone in this picture is not having fun. What is that big boy doing? Why isn't it fun when someone tries to hurt you or make you cry?

Doing Good Things with My Hands

Growing God's Way: God wants us to learn to use our hands to do good things.

This is a special time of year. You can see that this boy and girl are making something to give away. It wouldn't be fun to make a lot of valentines to keep, would it? Since they have some good friends, they want to send them valentines. But they think it is more fun to make the valentines than to buy them. What do you think?

WHAT DO YOU SEE?
How do you know this is not Christmas? How do you know it is February? How do you know the boy and girl are making valentines instead of buying them?

A TIME TO SHARE
1. How many valentines do you see?
2. What else do you see that helped the boy and girl make the valentines? Can you name each thing they used and tell how it helped make the valentines?
3. Why does God want us to learn to use our hands? What good things can we do for Him with our hands?

WHAT YOU SHOULD KNOW ABOUT THIS BOOK

GROWING GOD'S WAY TO SEE AND SHARE is a book about growing up. All boys and girls do that. But not all boys and girls grow God's way. In this book there are 174 experiences that help your child grow God's way. These not only tell your child about the growing up experiences, but show them how others have fun as they grow God's way. Growing God's way is presented as delightful times with family and friends. When your child reads about these fun experiences, he or she will want to do them, and thank God for them.

Childhood

Childhood is not merely preparation for adult life, although that is one important function. We must recognize the value of childhood for the sake of childhood as well as its important preparation for adult living.

God had a wonderful idea when He planned for us to go through childhood. It was His idea, you know. He could have planned it in such a way that we would enter the world as mature adults and live out the full term as adults. But He didn't. God thought it good that we become children first.

Childhood as Preparation for Adult Living

We all recognize the value of growing into adult living. We grow slowly, accepting more and more responsibility and we become increasingly capable of handling larger tasks. This slow growth and slow positioning toward responsibility keeps us from facing enormous demands overnight.

God planned growth through age levels of childhood from infancy to adulthood. Step by step we move through each important stage of growth. At each stage we expect to accomplish certain things which

are characteristic of that age level.

Caring parents go beyond the basic demands of an age level and provide a rich assortment of experiences which help their child mature more rapidly than his peers. But the wise parent keeps these experiences somewhat within the child's level of growth, giving a child more and better experiences for his own level of growth, but not trying to force the child to perform far beyond his age level.

Growth regarded as normal for each level is best experienced at that level. Except for a gifted child, we expect two-year-olds to grow as twos, not as ten-year-olds. And we expect ten-year-olds to grow as tens, not as twos.

Maturity in adult life comes from fulfilling important maturing experiences at each age level. We must never accept the idea that childhood is less important than adulthood merely because a child appears to be a "little kid." In the total tapestry of life, what is accomplished at the age of two is as important as what is accomplished at the age of twenty-two, or thirty-two, or sixty-two.

Childhood for the Sake of Childhood

Preparation for adult living is an important part of childhood. But childhood for the sake of childhood is equally important. Or to put it another way, childhood is important not only for what we can get out of it, but also for what we can put into it.

If we always look on childhood as only a way leading somewhere (toward adulthood), we will miss those marvelous delights of childhood itself. Let's help our children enjoy being children, and let's find our delight in seeing them do that. Being a child is as important as becoming an adult. When we accept that, we accept a child as a total person, not as an incomplete one.

The Erosion of Childhood

Society is too often not in tune with this idea. Childhood becomes a means to an end—growing up and getting into adult productivity. Thus, the faster we get to adulthood, the better it is.

is almost always building a relationship with someone—father, mother, grandfather, grandmother, uncle, aunt, teacher, neighbor, friend, and others.

Read-to-Me

Another part of the togetherness emphasis is the read-to-me nature of this book. This book will do its work best when parent or teacher reads to the child. The read-to-me experience is one of togetherness, of feeling the warmth of presence, hearing a loving voice, talking with someone the child loves, and knowing that person is there to share this delightful experience with him. Read-to-me is a two-way street, with parent or teacher reaching out to share while the child reaches out to listen and learn.

Because of the strong read-to-me emphasis, this book uses oral vocabulary rather than the child's "learning to read" vocabulary. It also uses imagery and sentences more often associated with oral communication rather than those associated with beginning reading.

Tense Change

Occasionally you will encounter a deliberate change of tense within a "story," especially in the Bible material. This recognizes a past action along with the child's involvement in a current happening. It helps to involve your child now in an event pictured in the past, or a past action which led to the pictured scene.

Picture Reading

The primary emphasis of the storytelling portion is picture reading. Instead of reading a story, you read a picture. Out of that, you and your child discover a story. The story unfolds as you look at the picture and "read" it together.

As you read each picture together, you will discover something that helps your child grow God's way. Because these new discoveries are fun times, your child will want to do them, and by doing them he or she will grow God's way.

Picture reading is a blend of the visual and the verbal, helping you and your child enter into true-to-life experiences vicariously as you sit together in your living room or Sunday School room.

Discovery Power

With each picture is a question and answer feature called WHAT DO YOU SEE? It focuses on the little things in the picture which you may easily pass by too quickly. By finding and focusing on these little things, you and your child develop "discovery power" which

may be used in everyday life. It will help you discover those little things we pass by too quickly every day. And it will help you find meaning in each one.

Discovery power helps your child become more observant. He or she will look for clues that will tell why the scene is one season instead of another, or why it is one room rather than another, or why it is one time of the day instead of another.

Discovery power also encourages and stimulates imagination, observation, and creativity. These are the